FRIEDRICH FROEBEL AND
ENGLISH EDUCATION

Friedrich Froebel

FRIEDRICH FROEBEL
and
English Education

P. WOODHAM-SMITH

J. P. SLIGHT,   O. B. PRIESTMAN

H. A. HAMILTON,   N. ISAACS

Edited by
EVELYN LAWRENCE

PHILOSOPHICAL LIBRARY
NEW YORK

Published 1953 by the Philosophical Library Inc.,
15 East Fortieth Street,
New York 16, N.Y.

PRINTED AND BOUND IN GREAT BRITAIN FOR THE PHILOSOPHICAL LIBRARY INC.
BY HAZELL WATSON AND VINEY LTD., AYLESBURY AND LONDON

PREFACE

THE Governing Body of the National Froebel Foundation considered that the centenary of Froebel's death should not be allowed to pass without some attempt to assess the achievement of the Froebel movement in this country. In particular it seemed worth while to bring together the scattered records of its history before the last remaining memory links with earlier pioneers are dissolved.

A seven-year-old child once wrote: "The Ancient Britons are dead and it's all through the Romans." The last thing which the Foundation wishes to claim is that advances in primary school education are "all through Froebel". This book is merely an attempt at such stock-taking as is possible.

The Foundation brought together a group of contributors who formed themselves into a committee and jointly planned the book, with the valuable help and advice of Dr. A. V. Judges, Professor of the History of Education in the University of London. There was considerable discussion of the work in progress, but the author of each chapter worked in general independently, and each is responsible for the views expressed. No attempt was made to impose an artificial uniformity of outlook among the writers, but it was found that there was wide agreement on most important issues.

The writer of the historical chapters wishes to express her thanks to the Principals of the Froebel Educational Institute, the Maria Grey Training College, Stockwell College and the Norland Institute, also to the Headmistress of Highbury Hill High School and the Secretary of the Sesame Club for permission to use their records, and to Miss Grace Owen for much valuable information

5

about the beginnings of the Froebel movement in Manchester and about the Blackheath and Mather Training Colleges. The staff of the National Froebel Foundation and the librarians of the Ministry of Education and the Maria Grey College have also been very kind in tracing books and other relevant material.

We are indebted for the illustrations to the London County Council, *Picture Post* and the Principal of the Froebel Educational Institute. In addition, the portrait of Froebel and the reproduction of the title-page of *The Education of Man* were kindly supplied by Dr. Erika Hoffmann, Principal of the Evangelisches Froebel-seminar, Kassel. Dr. Hoffmann has also provided valuable information relating to present-day opinion in Germany about Froebel's own background and doctrine.

EVELYN LAWRENCE

National Froebel Foundation
2 Manchester Square
London, W.1

CONTENTS

CONTRIBUTORS

MISS P. WOODHAM-SMITH, M.A.
Late Deputy-Principal, Maria Grey Training College.

MISS J. P. SLIGHT, B.Sc.
Late Schools' Adviser, Kesteven (Lincolnshire) Education Committee (formerly adviser to Leeds Education Committee). Author of *Living With Our Children*.

MISS O. B. PRIESTMAN, B.A.
N.F.U. Teacher's Certificate. Headmistress of Ibstock Place School, Roehampton. Author of *Froebel Education Today*.

THE REV. H. A. HAMILTON, B.A.
Principal of Westhill Training College, Selly Oak, Birmingham. Author of *The Family Church*, *Christian Education Handbooks* and *Christian Youth Training*.

NATHAN ISAACS, O.B.E.
Author of *Children's Why Questions* (in Susan Isaacs' *Intellectual Growth in Young Children*) and of *The Foundations of Common Sense*.

MISS EVELYN LAWRENCE, B.Sc., Ph.D.
Director, National Froebel Foundation. Author of *Intelligence and Inheritance*.

INTRODUCTION

A HUNDRED years after Froebel's death it is instructive to look back over the century and to consider how far and in what directions his ideas have travelled, within a country where they were welcomed: and perhaps to ask ourselves why they travelled at all. With the history of influences we are always on perilous ground. The original doctrine is there to be scrutinised, and we can analyse it afresh. But why it caught on, to what degree and with whom, who helped it to grow and who tried to stamp it out, how far it modified or was itself modified by other beliefs—these questions can never be more than partially determined. The history of education is a complex one, like the history of life itself. The forgotten teachers in their classrooms, the innumerable lectures, magazine articles, conferences and drawing-room meetings are gone mostly without record. Generalised stages in educational change do not readily suggest themselves, but after a century of evolution the scene has altered and its modifications can be noted.

It is impossible to describe the schools of a country like England as if they were uniform. There is no centrally imposed curriculum or method; teachers are left free to work according to their own lights and the needs of their pupils, and the greater or lesser exigencies of an always impoverished service. So one can notice only what the best schools are like now, how many of that kind can be found, and what proportion of the dreary repressive type remain. We may be tempted to remark that we are in a transition phase. But the transition phase is perennial. The theoretical battle that raged a century ago rages today, but mainly not among the leaders. Most of those were won over long since, at any rate in the field of the primary school. And we can safely say that Froebel and his followers played a leading part in such improvement as there has been.

In this book of essays it has not been possible to do more than offer a brief account of the man, his beliefs and his work, of the kind of places the better schools are today, and of the people and events which have formed the link between Froebel in 1852 and English education in 1952. To give fuller meaning to the story Froebel's philosophy and his views about children are examined critically, in the light of a hundred years' development in psychology and in educational theory. Unfortunately space could not be found for an examination of the philosophic antecedents of Froebel's own doctrines. We are here concerned however with the history of those doctrines in England, and how he came by them is not perhaps as important now as how he developed them. Moreover, it is very hard to discover how he did come by them. His autobiography, his other writings and those of his contemporaries about him refer hardly at all to his reading, nor mention contacts with leading thinkers of his day. Apart from the influence of Rousseau via Pestalozzi it seems that there was little beyond the general romantic-liberal-idealist spirit of the times in which he lived. The rest was his own ardent mind shaping and re-shaping his thoughts about man and the universe.

But what makes a man a great educational reformer, and how does it come about that his ideas are spread abroad in a way which changes the day-by-day practice in the ordinary school? It cannot be merely the rightness of his views. Many people have been right and unregarded. It must be in each case a unique combination of circumstances—the nature of his ideas, the way he expresses them, the social problems which are receiving attention in his time, and the kind of disciples who happen to come under his influence. Probably no widespread movement can be permanently successful without a group of followers round the leader who can bring strength and initiative of their own to the campaign, and revolutionary fire to reinforce that of their master. And there is also needed a kind of little propagating cell where pockets of this fire are kept alive and nourished, here and there to be fanned and to join up into a wider blaze. All these Froebel had. The cells were the schools themselves and the little Froebel groups that grew up all over the place. These meant that ideas were fairly quickly embodied in action, and in equipment and buildings, none of which can vanish in a breath as words can.

If we consider Froebel himself, we find all the makings of a prophet. Besides the fervour and the personal magnetism, the conviction of rightness and the self-confidence needed in a leader, he seems to have had an endearing quality which some prophets lack, and his way with children inspired and greatly moved those who saw it. Then the nature of what he taught would make the strongest possible appeal to very many people. They were invited to contemplate children, and what could be lovelier things to contemplate? The holiness of God, the beauty and grandeur of nature, "the army of unalterable law", the order and symmetry of a living yet mathematical universe, wisdom and service, love and gaiety, all were brought together in one great simple scheme. Moreover, his basic views, the background of his system, were expressed very generally so that each reader or listener could fill them out with his own individual vision, and they remained true for people of very different levels of understanding and imagination. The dull details of his scholastic method were given a rosy halo by reflections from the wider glory; and anyway they were so much better than the kind of things done in the mass-production schools of countries fighting their first great war with illiteracy, that as a stage in educational development we cannot disparage them.

So Froebel found disciples in Germany to help him with his schools and the training of teachers and with the general propaganda work which soon spread his doctrines widely. Then when after the failure of the 1848 revolution the liberal groups were scattered, those who came to England found a ready response among several different sections of the community here. There was a sprinkling of rich, cultured and public-spirited upper-middle class people, Manchester merchants and the like, who cared about education, both for their own children and for those of the proletarian masses. Education for the latter could come only slowly. Even if the country had not been determined to get its education cheaply, it would take years to find, let alone train, enough teachers for universal schooling on liberal lines. But at any rate the children of the poor were not entirely left out of the discussion. Some members of the wealthy Jewish community encouraged the movement with the greatest generosity. Then the group of powerful pioneering women who were fighting for higher education for women and public school education for girls found the new doctrine to their taste. Perhaps the titles of the Baroness von Marenholtz Bülow and others whose sympathies were enlisted over here, together with the glamour of various royal personages who were interested, also helped to give the movement prestige.

So rank and wealth reinforced the widespread reforming zeal already at work, and the new ideas grew and spread as the century progressed. Official opinion here and there added its authority and allowed breaches to be made in the entrenchment of the national system.

The welcome given to the German leaders of the movement was cordial and reminds twentieth century readers who have lived through two wars with Germany that the two countries have not always been, and need not be enemies. For some reason the German women came to be known in England as Madame—Madame Michaelis, Madame de Portugall—which gives the earlier Froebel period a slightly exotic flavour. But half a century saw Froebelianism thoroughly naturalised here.

Anglo-Saxons on the whole like to think for themselves, and they do not often want all to do the same thing at the same time. Neither do they want this for their children. So gradually the more formal parts of the school method were dropped, and freedom and initiative for the children, in accordance with Froebel's own better teaching, crept in. Gradually the movement broadened out as more teachers were trained and more Froebel schools were established. Among more progressive educationists Froebel's main principles became part of the ordinary stuff of thinking, no longer necessarily attached to the name of the man who gave them birth. Froebel has become history, and if you don't like history you don't have to know about Froebel. But you cannot do without his ideas.

Some people, however, do still fight against Froebel's ideas. It is a matter partly of judgment, partly of temperament. The subtle adjustments needed for a method based on giving scope for the movements of other minds, the rhythms of other lives, the initiative of other wills, are not easy for every teacher. The theory takes some understanding, and the method some mastering. Certain people are temperamentally hostile to it. They like to dominate, or they fear a system which is not neat, cut and dried. They prefer to be anchored continuously to textbooks, to prepared lessons and safe syllabuses and timetables. Others reflect on the vast quantities of knowledge which are there to be imparted, and assiduously cut it up into little chunks and feed it in, unable to trust the children's spontaneous appetites. Yet, again, freer methods have to be defended from some of their wilder friends. Many teachers have taken one look into the bear-garden which a "free" school can become in the wrong hands, and have returned in horror, the more moderate ones to their mark lists and formal lessons, the diehards to their detentions and their canes.

It must be admitted that a great deal of theoretical work still remains to be done by those who have no doubts about the rightness of Froebel's basic doctrines. For instance we are not yet very clear about the degree of freedom which is best in the hour-by-hour class room situation for children of different temperaments, ages and levels of intelligence; and again there are various opinions concerning how far the fields of knowledge should be mapped out in orderly fashion for easier assimilation, how far they should be left for each child, with the teacher's help, to deal with in his own way. The problems are very numerous and very important, so that the need for research is as great as it ever was; and there is very little money, time or trained personnel for it. But many schools are experimenting, opportunities for publication of results have increased, and it has at last become respectable for university departments to concern themselves with the young child. In general the Ministry of Education and the Local Authorities are actively encouraging teachers to try out their own procedures. The post-war years have seen a real forward movement in spite of the tremendous handicaps imposed by bombed buildings, large classes and shortages of everything that the schools need. Even the pitched battles waged in the educational papers show that the issues are alive. We can perhaps be justified in hoping that, given peace, the pace of improvement in the schools will quicken, and that another century will not be necessary for securing the kind of education which a twentieth century Froebel would consider worthy.

CHAPTER I

THE ORIGIN OF THE KINDERGARTEN

In the year 1852, at Blankenburg in Thuringia, there died a man destined after his death and through the work of his devoted disciples to have an influence on educational thought and practice which was to become world wide. It was capable of such development that many of the theories which appeared revolutionary less than a hundred years ago are now so universally accepted that most people have forgotten their origin. It is indeed hard to believe that there was a time when those who held them had to fight for a hearing and for the right to put what they believed into practice.

Friedrich Froebel was not the first educator to attach importance to the education of little children; Renaissance writers, who mostly confined their writings to the education of a ruling class, had written of the importance of the right choice of nurse, mainly that the child might acquire correct speech and the accepted standard of morals. The great seventeenth century educator Comenius, whom Froebel in many ways resembled, was never in the position to carry out the curriculum he planned in the *Great Didactic*. He realised the importance of the child's early years, but he thought of the child under six years of age as being solely in the care of his mother; in his vernacular school, which was to be for both boys and girls between the ages of six and twelve, the children were to learn from the objects around them which they could see, touch and smell; they were to be encouraged to play, and they were to be taught to use their voices and their hands. In the eighteenth century, among Froebel's almost contemporaries, the Alsatian pastor Oberlin had for a time established infant schools in his efforts to bring civilisation to a remote parish in the Vosges, and this had an influence on the development of infant schools in France and Belgium. The great Swiss educators Père Girard and Pestalozzi, although revolutionary in their ideas, which included the training of teachers, and in their methods, placing the observation of natural objects and the use of the hands before book learning, believed that the place for young children was not the school but the home. Froebel not only saw that infants benefited by communal life, but by close observation built up a system based on their needs and allowing for their mental and spiritual growth. Conclusions were reached which led him to found the kindergarten towards the end of his life, and in order to understand how he came by them it is necessary to state briefly the main events in his life.

Friedrich Froebel was born in Oberweissbach, a village in the Thuringian forest on April 21st, 1782. He was the fifth son of the village pastor. His mother died when he was a few months old, and he was left to the care of servants and his elder brothers, for whom he had a very great and lasting affection. His father married again when he was four; his stepmother was kind to him until she had a child of her own; she then began to treat him with great unkindness. As a result he was much alone, for his elder brothers were no longer living at home, and he became in consequence introspective. He records that his father taught him to read, and that he succeeded in doing so only with very great difficulty. As soon as he could read he was sent to the village school, where he received a religious education in harmony with the teaching he received from his father's pulpit.

When he was nearly eleven years old he was removed from the unhappy atmosphere of his home by going to live with his uncle, his mother's brother, Superintendent

Hoffmann at Stadt-Ilm; there he met with kindness and sympathy, while his new school gave him the companionship of other boys. At Oberweissbach he had, at his father's desire, been placed in the girls' school.

He records that throughout his life he was always seeking for hidden connections and an underlying unity in all things, and that he failed to find it in the piecemeal studies of school.

In 1797, when he was a little over fifteen years of age, he was apprenticed to a forester. He was able to indulge and develop his love of nature and to gain a knowledge of plants, while he devoted his spare time to mathematics and languages. He was still much alone, and continued his habits of self-observation and introspection. In 1799, at the conclusion of his apprenticeship, he entered the University of Jena, where one of his brothers was studying medicine. He attended lectures on a variety of scientific subjects connected with forestry, and on pure mathematics for which he had an aptitude. He records that his residence at Jena taught him much. "I had won for myself a standpoint, both subjective and objective. I could already perceive unity in diversity, the correlation of forces, the inter-connection of all living things, life in matter, and the principles of physics and biology." [1] Through no fault of his own, he fell into debt and was for nine weeks in the university prison. His father paid his debt and secured his release on condition that he renounced all rights in the paternal inheritance. Upon his release he returned home but he never regained his father's confidence. His father died in 1802. Froebel once more left home and was again employed in forestry and land surveying.

The uncle who had rescued him in boyhood died in 1805 and left him a small legacy. With this he went to Frankfurt with the intention of studying architecture.

---

[1] *Autobiography*, translated Michaelis and Moore.

This proved to be the turning-point in his life, for he was introduced to Herr Gruner, a pupil of Pestalozzi and headmaster of Frankfurt Model School. He persuaded Froebel to become a teacher in his school, and before taking up the post to visit Yverdun.

This first visit lasted only a fortnight; he returned impressed although critical of what he had seen and heard, and he was determined some day to pay a second visit.

At Frankfurt he taught arithmetic, drawing, geography and German to the middle classes of the school, and he felt that in teaching he had at last found his true vocation. He wrote to his brother: "It seemed as if I had found something I had never known but always longed for, always missed, as if my life had at last discovered its native element. I felt as happy as the fish in the water, the bird in the air." [1]

It was the custom in the school for each master to take his pupils for a walk once a week and employ the time in the way he thought most useful. Froebel began by using his walk for botanising, but turned to geography and made with his pupils the type of survey we should nowadays term environmental study.

In addition to his work in the school he undertook the tutorship of three private pupils. This forced him to think out his own theory of education. Before long he gave up his school appointment to become their full-time tutor; in doing so he stipulated with their parents that they should live in the country, and that they should be handed over to his sole care. He began by devoting most of their time to nature study and gardening.

The following year, 1808, he went with them to Yverdun, where they remained for two years. Froebel entered fully into the life of the institution, and enjoyed and found stimulating the society of the young men

[1] *Autobiography.*

drawn from many nations whom the fame of Pestalozzi had drawn round him. He acknowledged that these years were critically decisive for his later life and that he learnt much during them; that music and singing had been brought before him as a means of human culture, that the study of the boys' games in the open air had taught him "to recognise their mighty power to awaken and to strengthen the intelligence and the soul as well as the body," [1] and that "closely akin to the games in their morally strengthening aspect were the walks, especially the general walking parties, more particularly when conducted by Pestalozzi himself." [1] These walks always afforded opportunities of drawing close to nature, even when this was not the purpose of the walk.

As in his former visit, he was critical of what he saw; much as he admired Pestalozzi he was not altogether at one with him; he deplored the lack of system in which the institution was conducted and the jealousies and lack of harmony among those who surrounded the great teacher. He wrote at the close of his visit: "I felt more clearly than ever the deficiency of inner unity and inter-dependence, as well as of outward comprehensiveness and thoroughness in the teaching there." [1]

He decided that as soon as he had returned his pupils to their home he would again enter a university, for he had reached the conclusion that a knowledge of natural science was indispensable for an educator.

In 1811 he entered the University of Göttingen, hoping to find through study "that unity which was so necessary to me, between my inward and my outward life, and the equally necessary harmony between aim, career and method".[1]

"Mankind as a whole, as one great unity, had now become my quickening thought," [1] he wrote, and this thought led him for a time to linguistic studies; he became

---

[1] *Autobiography.*

enthralled with the study of Greek, but he soon returned to his original intention of studying natural science. Physics, chemistry, mineralogy and natural history were his principal studies, and from these he passed to organic chemistry and geology; and as he wished to compare the laws of Nature with the laws of Man, he added history, politics and political economy.

In 1812 he decided to move to Berlin, where he could study crystallography, mineralogy and natural history under Professor Weiss and at the same time obtain some teaching himself.

So far Froebel's life had been singularly undisturbed by the events which were shaking Europe, but this move was to bring him for a time into the maelstrom of war. The University of Berlin had recently been founded to take the place of Halle, which had fallen under Napoleonic influence after the crushing defeat of Prussia at Jena in 1806; it was natural that the students should be enthusiastic for the overthrow of Napoleon, and eager to enlist when Prussia declared war on France after the retreat from Moscow. Froebel was no Prussian, but he was conscious of German brotherhood, and joined in 1813 a famous volunteer corps in which he saw some military service. This is important, because he made three friends, two of whom helped materially in his later work—Langethal and Middendorff.

At the conclusion of hostilities he returned to Berlin, where he remained for two years acting as assistant at the Mineralogical Museum.

His determination to devote himself to education strengthened with the passage of time, and, realising that language was the expression of thought, he turned his attention again to the classical languages; but more and more the thought possessed him that "the one thing needful for man was unity of development, perfect evolution in accordance with the laws of his being, such evolution as science discovers in the other organisations of nature."[1]

In 1816 he was called upon to put his theories into practice. Between the years 1813 and 1816 two of his brothers had died, and he decided to undertake the education of their children. He opened a school at Griesheim and called upon his friends Middendorff and Langethal to come and help him. Two years later the school was moved to Keilhau. Here Froebel carried out some of the ideas which had been formulating in his mind for so long. The same year he married, and a few years later Middendorff married one of his nieces and Langethal his wife's adopted daughter. In 1831 Middendorff's nephew Barop, who was destined to carry on Froebel's work at Keilhau, married yet another niece; so the friends became united by family relationship.

The "new education" progressed slowly; the little community was often hard put to it for money and even for food, but in the course of time it won its way, and boys were sent to receive an education in which the training of character and the observation of nature, which included work on the land, were regarded as of more importance than facility in reading the classical languages.

Froebel wrote constantly on educational matters, until in 1826 he published what was destined to be the most famous of his writings—*The Education of Man*. In it he emphasised the importance of character as opposed to book learning, of permitting the human being to develop in accordance with nature. "Every human being, even as a child, must be recognised, acknowledged, and fostered as a necessary and essential member of humanity, and so the parents should feel and recognise themselves responsible as fosterers to God, to the child, and to humanity."[1]

[1] *Autobiography.*

He likened the growth of the child to the growth of a plant, to be tended and cared for as the gardener cares for his seedlings, and he emphasised the importance of play for the young child, leading to purposeful activity in the classroom. Above all, education should lead to harmony with God and nature.

Four years later Froebel attempted to found a second school in Switzerland. This was a failure owing to local opposition, but he was brought into contact with young teachers in the canton of Lucerne to whom he lectured, and became himself the head of an orphan asylum at Burgdorf. He found that until children reached school age they were often totally neglected so far as their minds and characters were concerned. He had already come to the conclusion from his experiences at Keilhau that the children who came to him at the age of nine or ten often had bad habits of both conduct and methods of learning so ingrained that it was difficult to eradicate them; and his thoughts turned more and more to the importance of the early years of childhood and the way in which children should be treated during those early years. He began to plan a graduated course of exercises modelled on the games in which they were most interested. In Switzerland, too, he realised the importance of training for all those who had to do with young children, whether they were mothers, teachers or nurses.

On his return to Keilhau in 1837, he opened the first kindergarten or garden of children in the neighbouring village of Blankenburg. He attached a great deal of importance to finding the right name for this institution; he rejected the term "infant school" because it was not to be a school; children were not to be schooled but freely developed. He rejected various other names, including "Nursery School for Little Children"; finally he hit upon the name with a shout—"Eureka! I have found it, kindergarten it shall be called."

He began to work out the series of toys or apparatus which became known as the "Gifts" and "Occupations". The purpose of the gifts was to provide for the children's play, but at the same time to train them in dexterity of movement and to teach them something of the laws of nature. They consisted of balls, blocks for building, coloured tablets for design, coloured papers to cut and fold, clay and sand, pencils and paints, arranged in a series. The occupations consisted of paper folding, perforated paper designs for pricking, drawing on squared paper, intertwining, weaving, folding, cutting, peawork, cardboard and clay modelling.[1]

True to his belief that music formed an important part in education, Froebel published in 1843 *Mutter und Kose-Lieder*, a collection of action songs and singing games based on folk music and the occupations and objects which the children saw around them.

Above all, the kindergarten should be "child centred". "My teachers are the children themselves with their purity and innocence, their unconsciousness, and their irresistible claims, and I follow them like a faithful, trustful scholar," [2] he wrote to his cousin Frau Schmidt when she was about to open a kindergarten at Gera. "It is of no consequence that precisely these songs and these tunes shall be sung which have been suggested by myself; they have been put forward merely by way of example; others may find some prettier and more suitable." [2]

A second kindergarten in Rudolstadt was opened in 1840, and both Froebel and Middendorff lectured on the scheme in Dresden, Frankfurt, Hamburg and elsewhere. Froebel also gave an account of his plans in a weekly paper which circulated from 1837 to 1840. The original kindergarten had to be given up, partly through lack of funds, partly to give Froebel and Middendorff more time

---

[1] See Appendix.   [2] *Letters.*

for their propaganda tours. The training of kindergarten teachers continued first at Keilhau, and from 1848 until the time of Froebel's death, at Liebenstein in the Thuringian forest and at Marienthal in the Duchy of Meiningen. The students were mainly young girls, for he had come to the conclusion that young women because of their strong maternal instincts made, when trained for the work, the best teachers of young children.

His devoted wife, who had suffered ill health for some years, died in 1839; in 1851, less than a year before his death, realising that his establishment needed a woman head, Froebel married again, a pupil, Luise Levin, who was destined to be one of the faithful disciples who carried on his work after his death.

His last days were saddened by the news that kindergartens, of which there were about twenty all told, were prohibited in the kingdom of Prussia owing to the confusion of Froebel with a nephew who had engaged in socialist propaganda.

In the long run, the suppression of liberalism in the German states after the abortive attempts at revolution in 1848 benefited the kindergarten movement, for it led to a widespread emigration of liberal-minded Germans to America and to Western European countries, and in many cases, notably in America and England, the children of these emigrants became the first pupils of kindergartners who were seeking to promote Froebel's ideas beyond the limits of their own country. But Froebel did not live to see this happen; he died on June 21st, 1852.

Middendorff died the following year, and Barop became the headmaster of the school at Keilhau. Frau Luise Froebel went to Hamburg in the autumn of 1854 as directress of the Public Free Kindergarten. She trained students there for many years, receiving a pension from the Empress Frederick when she grew too old to work.

Baroness von Marenholtz-Bülow

Madame Michaelis

The most important of those who undertook propaganda work for the kindergarten, or as R. H. Quick so aptly termed Froebel's teaching, "The New Education", was the Baroness Bertha von Marenholtz-Bülow. She first met Froebel in 1849 while visiting the Baths at Liebenstein. Froebel had established himself on a small farm at Liebenstein, and was training a class of young women to become kindergartners. He had also gained some notoriety for the lack of self-consciousness with which he played games with the children of the neighbourhood. The Baroness became interested in the work, and made a point of spending some time with Froebel and Middendorff during her annual visit to the Baths. She was the means of interesting many important people in the movement and of introducing it to the court circles of Weimar and Meiningen. It was through her influence that Froebel was given the use of the shooting-box at Marienthal.

In her *Reminiscences of Froebel* she recorded "the foundation of all his discourses was always his theory of development—the law of universal development applied to the human being".[1] She wrote too of the devotion which he engendered in his pupils. "How very much Froebel did influence the moral culture of his pupils is made public by the unbounded love and gratitude expressed by the majority of them at the time of his death. . . . the new truth concerning the nature of childhood which he brought out cannot be without influence upon all branches of education: and here it was that Froebel knew no yielding whenever the jewel of truth entrusted to him was questioned or attacked."[1]

She acknowledged that Froebel was often obscure. "He was most difficult to understand when he spoke of the application of his 'law' through the gifts; and also when he treated of the first impressions of the outward

---

[1] Bülow, *Reminiscences of Froebel.*

world upon the very young child, which were given by concrete things, symbols as it were, for the later apprehension of spiritual facts." She considered Middendorff to be his best interpreter. It was "his deep and, for a man, rare sensibility that gave him so great a power to influence the female mind, and made him the best interpreter of Froebel's genius. What Froebel created was adopted by Middendorff, worked out with deepest devotion and generally given back in an intelligible form."

The Baroness Bertha von Marenholtz—she added her maiden name of Bülow at a later date—was the second wife of the Baron von Marenholtz, a member of the Privy Council in Brunswick and afterwards Court Marshal in Hanover.

She brought up her stepdaughters, who showed her great affection, but her only child, a son named Alfred, died at an early age after a long illness, which the Baroness felt was due to the severity of his education. According to her niece and biographer her enthusiasm for what she often termed "the cause" was largely due to her determination that other children should not suffer as Alfred had suffered. "That all children should be protected from what her own child had had to suffer was the task to which my aunt had pledged herself over the body of her Alfred, and an unbroken apostleship of forty years for the new theory of education was the fulfilment of her vow."

After Froebel's death, the training of teachers was moved from Marienthal to Keilhau, and there the Baroness met Langethal and Barop, and also two of Middendorff and Frau Froebel's pupils, Thekla Naveau and Eleonore Heerwart; the latter was destined to play an important part in the spread of the kindergarten in the British Isles.

It was Middendorff who advised the Baroness to carry the propaganda abroad; he who at the time of Froebel's death had replied to her "Whatever will become of the Cause?" with "A truth never will be lost".

The Baroness horrified her relations by her proposal to carry on propaganda abroad, and indeed, in a period when the women of the upper classes were not in the habit of travelling alone or of staying in hotels, and when it was very rare for a woman to speak in public, her project seemed daring in the extreme. However, accompanied sometimes in her early travelling years by a friend and later by the niece who wrote her biography, she carried out a series of lecturing tours.

Her first journey was to England in the summer of 1854, and from there she crossed to Paris, where she knew no one and had no introductions.

She remained in France for the greater part of three years. There were already some crèches in existence, and at one of these the patroness, the Empress Eugénie, allowed a trial to be made of Froebel's methods. After three months the investigating committee pronounced a favourable opinion, so that during the second year of the Baroness's stay the "Comité du Patronage des Jardins d'Enfants" was founded.

Her propaganda was not without personal discomfort —"for hours she would go without food, as being a lady, and alone, she could not well go into a public restaurant."

In 1857 she attended a great International Charity Congress at Frankfurt-on-Main, where she delivered lectures in French and German, and in consequence received many invitations to visit European countries. The same year she went to Belgium and Holland. Madame Guillaume, a kindergarten teacher from Hamburg who had married in Brussels, had recently established a kindergarten; it is interesting to note that the French socialist Proudhon, an exile in that city, moved his home in order that his children might attend the kindergarten.

The campaign in Holland was rendered easy by the fact that Amélie, the daughter of the Duchess Ida von Weimar, who had known Froebel and who had done much to establish kindergartens in Weimar, had married Prince Heinrich of the Netherlands.

The Baroness's friend Frau von Calear, an authoress, did all she could to promote the "Cause" by working in Holland for thirty-five years to establish kindergartens and by translating German writings into Dutch.

From her it can be learnt that the Baroness's speaking was always extemporary. She wrote: "I see her still in my mind as I once saw her appear in Brussels, or more especially in the Grand Hôtel du Louvre in Paris, and lastly again in the royal palace in Amsterdam, surrounded by strangers from all nations, who had come at first in small numbers, mostly out of curiosity to hear a woman speak, but soon eager to hear more and more from her—and she left them fully convinced of the truth of the doctrine of this philosopher, who will probably one day be called the greatest thinker of his time. Often as I have heard her speak she never repeated herself, no matter where she began, or what aspects of the 'Cause' she touched upon. She always showed us the 'Cause' from another point of view, and clad its praise in another form. . . . How deeply she enabled us to see the germs of capacity in the child, the innermost secrets of his being, and thereby to feel the duty of every woman to deal with youth in an educational and pedagogic manner, because the child is an active person (individual), that must not be left in inaction, but must be always nourished by means of all the impressions made by the outer world. But no less clearly did she explain that the *maternal instinct* is not capable of educating a being to its moral distinction as a whole man, if this maternal instinct be not prepared by a proper training."

Froebel's four years in Switzerland had left no tangible results, but the system was reintroduced between 1856 and 1860. Professor Raoux of Lausanne established a kindergarten in his house in 1859, from which the methods spread in the French-speaking cantons in spite of a lack of French-speaking teachers. In 1860 the Baroness visited kindergartens in Lausanne, Geneva and Neuchâtel. She had on an earlier occasion visited Zürich.

In 1860 the ban was removed from the kindergartens in Prussia. The Baroness had been in the habit of giving lectures to ladies in her own house in Berlin whenever she was at home, and in 1859 a Women's Association was formed; and as soon as it was possible to establish kindergartens, two of Froebel's pupils, Fräulein Ida Steele and Fräulein Kramer, came to Berlin to direct the two kindergartens of the association. An association for the training of teachers was also formed. To the students of this institution the Baroness herself gave the instruction in Froebel's theory of education.

By this means the movement spread to Finland and to Russia, for the Grand Duchess Hélène, who was keenly interested in developing education, sent three girls to Berlin for training.

A second conference was held in Frankfurt in 1869, which was followed by the publication of the Baroness's lectures, and in 1870, owing to differences with the Berlin association, she moved to Dresden, where she again gave lectures in her own house, which were attended for the most part by teachers. Her niece gives the following account of her lecturing: "My aunt possessed a most marvellous gift for teaching; I believe that few who had been fortunate enough to attend her lectures or lessons will ever forget them. In her beautiful, pure Hanoverian German, with a voice bright and clear . . . However deep her thought, her delivery was always most simple, and always clear, logical, convincing, enchanting. How many times have I been assured by pupils from far and near that my aunt's lectures not only inspired them for everything great, good and beautiful, but that they were so far prevailed upon by these lectures as to remain faithful for ever to the hard profession of teaching, and this with unconquerable enthusiasm."

Her work in Berlin was carried on by Froebel's great-niece Frau Schrader-Breymann, who had been one of the last students he trained. She became in 1873 the first Principal of the Pestalozzi-Froebel House, which still exists and which has for its object the training of girls in kindergarten methods and domestic science.

In 1871 took place the first meeting of the Allgemeine Erziehungs Verein at Dresden, an association by which it was hoped that the numerous kindergartens and the various efforts which were being made to train teachers and to disseminate Froebel's principles might be kept in touch with one another.

The Baroness's next journey was to Italy, where the ground had been well prepared for her. Italians had already met her in Paris and in Switzerland, articles in Swiss papers had been read in Italy, and in consequence the "gifts" and "occupations" were to be found in both North and South Italy; although in some cases the apparatus had been adopted without much understanding of the principles which lay behind it.

Kindergartens had been established in Rome, Naples, Palermo, Milan and Venice, and in Chambéry and Nice in the former Duchy of Savoy.

The revival of Italian life which was part of the liberation movement, and which showed itself in all directions, led to a desire to improve schools; and the recognition of how much depended on the beginnings of education led Garibaldi to create an association for the establishment of crèches and primary schools. This association of Italian women appealed for help to the many sympathisers with United Italy abroad.

During 1871–2 the Baroness visited Florence and some other cities including Rome, lecturing in her own room in her hotels, and in spite of some clerical opposition and the difficulty of German teachers speaking Italian, the movement flourished. Perhaps the most important outcome of this visit was her meeting with Mrs. Julie Salis-Schwabe, a friend of Garibaldi and a native of Hamburg, who was the wife of a wealthy Lancashire merchant and who had raised a large sum of money in England for welfare work among Italian children.

She had been interested in propagating the ideas of the British educationist William Ellis, founder of the William Ellis School, London, but the Baroness convinced her of the soundness of Froebel's principles, and at her request trained a young Italian teacher in his methods. Madame Schwabe was instrumental in founding an institution in Naples which had a marked influence in Southern Italy.

She began in 1873 with a kindergarten and elementary school, her object being to found a great institute which "should more adequately respond to the time and the greatest needs of the country and should form an organised whole of instruction and education, according to the methods of Froebel, where infants should be received, made to go through all the grades of primary instruction, and be taught some art or handicraft whereby to gain their livelihood".

At first she met with some prejudice, but in sixteen months the success, as far as numbers went, was assured, and by 1887 she had, in addition to the large sum of money with which she had endowed the institute, received grants from the Minister of Education and various public bodies. The same year it became a corporate body with the title of "Instituto Froebeliano Internazionale Vittorio Emanuele II".

The institution to which Madame Schwabe gave

much personal attention was first under a teacher trained in Dresden, but later was presided over by Madame de Portugall, who had been inspector of infant schools in the canton of Geneva where Froebel's methods were widely used. She had been trained in Berlin, had taught in Manchester and had been the examiner for the first examination of the London Froebel Society's certificate.

By 1889 there were 900 to 1,000 pupils in the institution, which consisted of five schools: a kindergarten for children of both sexes, a transitional class for children from six to seven, an elementary school for both sexes from seven to eleven or twelve years of age. Boys and girls at this stage were taught apart. A high school for girls admitted also pupils from other schools. They remained there until the age of seventeen or eighteen, when they could take a government examination. If they passed this and showed an aptitude for teaching, they could enter the Froebel Seminario or Normal School, where they were trained for a year in the theory and practice of Froebel's system. Girls from other schools, if they passed the government examination, were received for training. The kindergarten and transition classes were non-fee-paying, and the children received a dress and a school meal.

The Italian journey was the last long lecturing tour the Baroness undertook; increasing age made it necessary for her to spend most of her time in Germany, principally at the training institute which she had established in Dresden. Everyone who was interested in the movement made a point of visiting her at some time in their careers. This was not only true of European educationists, but also of those who were seeking to establish the kindergarten in the New World.

Dr. Henry Barnard, an American educationist, had been a delegate to an educational exhibition in London in 1854 at which the Baroness had lectured, and demonstrations had been given in their school by two teachers from Hamburg who had established a kindergarten in London.

Dr. Barnard wrote copiously and enthusiastically about the movement when he returned to America. His writings fired Miss Elizabeth Peabody with an attempt to found a kindergarten in Boston in 1860; and not content with the result of her own efforts, she proceeded to tour European kindergartens in 1867–8, and in the course of her tour visited the Baroness.

Upon her return to America she was instrumental with her sister, the widow of the educationist Horace Mann, in furthering the cause by writing and translating from German, by lecturing and by the formation of a Froebel Union.

Several German teachers had established isolated kindergartens in America; and after the Civil War was over the movement spread very rapidly.

The Baroness died in 1893; before her death it was possible for her to look back, wrote her niece, "from the height of her completed career on the established position and prospects of the New Education, to which she had devoted her life. . . . Wherever she looked in Europe the words 'Froebel's kindergarten' were not an empty sound, but had long ago become a fact—a recognised fact. Then she looked across the ocean to America and the kindergarten triumphed there."

CHAPTER II

HISTORY OF THE FROEBEL MOVEMENT IN ENGLAND

FOR a variety of reasons the British Isles proved suitable soil for the growth of the kindergarten movement. First of all, the infant school had been for over fifty years a reality, and often the object of philanthropy. This was due partly to the manner in which children had been employed in factories in the early stages of the Industrial Revolution, partly to the legislation which had at long last kept the younger of these children from such employment, necessitating someone caring for them while their parents and elder brothers and sisters were at work, and to the desire of many religiously minded people that they might learn to read in order that they might read the Bible. As a result, schools specifically for infants were established, at first by private subscription and after 1838 with government aid.

Secondly, pioneers of infant school teaching had not been wanting. One of these, Robert Owen (1771–1858), in the schools connected with his cotton mills at New Lanark had, between 1816 and 1824, established a school where young children were encouraged to play, to sing and to dance, to take an interest in natural objects and to understand the substance of a passage before they learnt to read. His efforts, and those of his supporters, led to the opening of infant schools in London and elsewhere. Later experimenters, such as Samuel Wilderspin and David Stow, developed schools which became increasingly didactic in tone, where the children's memories were exploited to the utmost and moral teaching was inculcated by every possible device. Although playgrounds were considered necessary and use was made of them, free movement was difficult in class-rooms which were encumbered by fixed platforms, arranged in tiers of steps and known as galleries; upon these the infants were required to sit, and to sit quietly, for all oral lessons.

It is important to remember that, although the teaching seemed to take so little notice of child nature, yet the infant school existed and was established in the public mind as a separate institution; and this in a period when older children were often attending school for the first time, and learning to read, write and add like their younger brothers and sisters. That young children should be considered to need a different approach is due largely to such associations as the Home and Colonial Society and the British and Foreign School Society, whose members were later to play an important part in supplying the country with kindergarten teachers.

The Home and Colonial Society was founded in 1837 for the purpose of training teachers, especially infant school teachers, in the principles of Pestalozzi. Pestalozzi believed that infants were best at home, taught by their own parents, but some of his adherents in England were interested in infant teaching and attempted to adapt his ideas to their own needs. The methods of Pestalozzi's pupil Fellenberg, who had a school at Hofwyl in Switzerland, were also known to many Englishmen, amongst them W. H. Herford of Manchester.

The views of a Swiss educator of an older generation, J. J. Rousseau, were well known in England, and had been disseminated in the writings of Thomas Day, Richard Lovell Edgeworth and, more especially, those of the latter's daughter Maria. Thus Froebel's spiritual antecedents were well known, at least to those who believed that education was something more than learning the three R's by rote; while the idea that the young child required different treatment in school from that given to older children, prepared the way for the acceptance of the "New Education" in the form of the kindergarten. In this connection it may be mentioned that for the children of the middle and upper classes, who in the first half of the nineteenth century were usually educated at home, a considerable literature had grown up. This, too, was didactic and highly moral, and included *Sandford and Merton* and Miss Edgeworth's collections of tales, such books as Mrs. Trimmer's *Story of the Robins*, Mrs. Sherwood's *The Fairchild Family* and Anne and Jane Taylor's *Original Poems for Infant Minds*—and many less well-known works.

Another important factor was the great increase in the number of German residents, particularly in London, Manchester and other great commercial centres, partly as a result of trade connections and largely because the reactionary governments set up in many German states after the failure of the revolution of 1848, led to the emigration of liberal-minded Germans to Great Britain and America. When in 1851 Johann and Bertha Ronge came to England and established a kindergarten in London, their pupils were at first all children of their own nationality. They record that their first English pupil was a nephew of Sir Rowland Hill. Readers may recollect that Sir Rowland Hill and his brothers had, at an earlier date, been the proprietors of a progressive boys' school, first in Birmingham and then at Bruce Grove in North London. In these schools self-government and handicrafts were important features.

Madame Ronge and her sister had been among Froebel's pupils in Hamburg in 1849. They were members of the wealthy Meyer family of North Germany, one of whose members, Heinrich Adolf Meyer, was described by the American educator and publicist Miss Elizabeth Peabody, writing about 1880, as "still the most enthusiastic patron of Froebel's kindergarten". Johann and Bertha Ronge had founded kindergartens in Germany before they came to London. Miss Margaretta Meyer came to England with her sister and worked with her until she married Mr. Carl Shutz and with him emigrated to America, where she founded the first American kindergarten in 1856 at Watertown, Wisconsin.

During the summer of 1854 the Baroness von Marenholtz-Bülow visited England. This was the first of her propaganda tours abroad. She was accompanied by the Countess Krockow von Wickerode, an Irishwoman whose maiden name was Elizabeth Micherly, who had first met the Baroness in 1841 and remained her devoted friend throughout her life. Her assistance was very necessary in London, for although the Baroness knew English, she had had very little opportunity of speaking the language; nevertheless, she showed indefatigable energy in furthering the "Cause". Teaching children in the Ragged Schools of London during the day and after school hours were over going hither and thither, often in the omnibuses which she dreaded, to meet persons who might be of importance to her scheme, spending the evenings in fashionable drawing-rooms—for "the foreign Baroness" was very much in request—she soon possessed a sufficient command of English to lecture, and when she entered a classroom the children greeted her with joy as "the stick lady".

Leading newspapers, such as *The Times* and the *Athenæum*, printed articles on the kindergarten; while Charles Dickens, who had met the Baroness and visited the Ronges' kindergarten, wrote a very full and informative article for his paper *Household Words*, while his sympathetic treatment of children and children's troubles in his subsequent novels helped to create a new attitude towards the child. The Bishop of Natal also met the Baroness, and asked her if the method was suitable for

Kaffir children. At his request she gave two teachers a short training before they sailed for South Africa.

In July 1854 the Society of Arts held an educational exhibition in St. Martin's Hall, opened by their President, the Prince Consort. To this the Baroness sent an exhibit of Froebel's gifts and occupations, which was demonstrated and explained by Herr Hoffmann, a pupil of Froebel's and the head of the training institution in Hamburg. At the same time the Ronge Kindergarten in Tavistock Place was thrown open to visitors. The exhibit created a great deal of interest, as did Heinrich Hoffmann's manner of exhibiting it; among those who have recorded their impressions were Dr. Henry Barnard, a delegate from Connecticut (see Chapter I), and the Rev. Muirhead Mitchell, H.M. Inspector of Church Schools in the Eastern Counties. Mr. Mitchell never ceased to commend teachers who employed kindergarten methods in the infant schools, and advised other teachers to get in touch with the Ronges to obtain the necessary apparatus.

In his annual report for 1854 he commended the Froebel apparatus as "among the few novelties" of the educational exhibition, and continued: "This system, though intellectual, is truly infantile; it treats the child as a child; encourages him to think for himself; teaches him, by childish toys and methods, gradually to develop in action or hieroglyphic writing his own idea, to tell his own story and to listen to that of others; there is no use of hard names, no singing of 'perpendicular' or 'horizontal', but whatever is said and whatever is done is totally and altogether such as belongs to a child."

The following year he commended the teaching given in St. Mark's School, Lakenham, Norfolk, probably by Miss Giles who is known to have demonstrated new methods to infant school teachers in Norfolk ten years later. He was convinced that infant school teachers should be differently selected and have a different training from the teachers of older children, and that this difference should not, as was often the case, take the form of expecting them to answer easier questions in the Certificate Examination, but that "her attention should be chiefly directed to the practical duties of her work, to improve her study of children's thoughts and actions, to ways of developing their intellects, to acquiring the different games and means whereby the attention of children is excited and maintained, to learning whether by note or ear or an instrument, the melodies and songs of childhood, and some study of the nature of the diseases to which they are subject, and such sanitary matters as mothers of the upper classes know well but too often of which the poorer classes are entirely ignorant, and which is the cause of much misery. A healthy frame, a good voice, a kindly, firm disposition, a graceful air, a pleasing manner, tidiness of person and sound general sense, are the necessary qualifications of those undertaking this work".

Mr. Mitchell recorded in the same report that he regarded museum cabinets of ores, shells, animal, vegetable and mineral production as of less use than toys and common objects. "A set of playthings, cups and saucers, a small kitchen with its implements really modelled on the life, a butcher's shop, a drawing-room and parlour, a bedroom and kitchen well furnished, might be made the means of conveying much more real and useful information than is contained in such cabinets. Furnished with such apparatus and two or three small dolls, how many agreeable and instructive incidents of life might not an intelligent teacher introduce to or act before her gallery of delighted children and not the less instructed because amused? Oh, what a dreary thing many a gallery lesson now is! I believe that the bulk of education and the happiness of the younger classes will be materially enhanced, if grants of pictures and toys were made by the Committee of Council to infant schools."

Although Mr. Mitchell does not seem to have been able to get away from the conception of an active teacher and a passive class, he had grasped the importance of child hygiene, and had caught the spirit of Froebel rather than the letter in realising that infants can learn from their ordinary toys and the common things of everyday life, at a time when his more orthodox followers were insisting on the correct manipulation of the gifts and occupations.

Before she left England the Baroness von Marenholtz-Bülow wrote a pamphlet, *Women's Educational Mission*, which was translated by her friend Countess Krockow von Wickerode and published in 1855. In it she recommended readers to purchase and read Johann and Bertha Ronge's *Practical Guide to the English Kindergarten*.

Heinrich Hoffmann remained in England after the exhibition closed to train teachers, and the Ronges also undertook training in their school. As a result, the kindergarten movement began to spread, and kindergartens or quasi-kindergartens were to be found in such cities as Manchester and Leeds. Professor Hoffmann seems to have returned to Germany for a time, but in 1857 he was invited by the Council of the Home and Colonial Society to direct the studies of the students in their institutions, of which there were two, one for infant school teachers in government-aided schools, the other established in 1846 with a school attached to it for the instruction of nursery governesses and teachers in higher class schools. In this work the Home and Colonial Society was a pioneer. Professor Hoffmann lectured to the infant school teachers in the one department, and was entirely responsible for the training of kindergarten teachers in the non-government section. A residence was provided for these students at 35, Mecklenburgh Square,

Die

Menschenerziehung,

die

Erziehungs-, Unterrichts-

und

Lehrkunst,

angestrebt

in

der allgemeinen deutschen Erziehungsanstalt

zu Keilhau;

dargestellt

von

dem Stifter, Begründer und Vorsteher derselben,

Friedrich Wilhelm August Fröbel.

Erster Band.
Bis zum begonnenen Knabenalter.

Keilhau 1826.
Verlag der allgemeinen deutschen Erziehungsanstalt.
Leipzig, in Commission bey A. Wienbrack.

The title-page of the original edition
of *The Education of Man*

while the training took place in the Gray's Inn Road, where a school was opened for practice and demonstration purposes. This department was instrumental in preparing, in addition to teachers in schools, a number of private governesses, and more especially teachers who intended to offer themselves as missionaries overseas. These missionaries, and those trained in America and sent out by American missionary societies, carried the kindergarten to the ends of the earth. In 1895 both the non-government department and the school were moved from the Gray's Inn Road to Highbury Hill.

After 1893 the Home and Colonial Society was incorporated in the National Froebel Union, for examination and certificate purposes so far as these non-government students were concerned. The Society also did good work in providing evening classes in kindergarten methods for infant school teachers.

Manchester was another interesting centre of educational activity. In 1857 Miss Barton, who had been trained by Madame Ronge, opened a kindergarten at 15, Cecil Street, Greenhays, and two years later she moved it to 9, Lime Grove. In the same year Johann and Bertha Ronge came to Manchester and gave an address on the "Kindergarten Educational System", and as a result the "Manchester Committee for the Extension of the Kindergarten System" was formed. Madame Ronge opened a school and training class at Whalley Range, and held classes for "teachers and ladies"; but she and her husband seem to have come up against the local committee on theological grounds, so in July 1860 they handed over the school to Mrs. Fretwell and her daughters, who had been trained by them and had a school in Leeds. Mrs. Fretwell appointed Madame de Portugall to conduct the Manchester school.

Madame de Portugall had studied the philosophical as well as the practical side of the kindergarten system, and was acquainted with both the Baroness and Froebel's great-niece, Frau Schrader-Breymann. She remained for two years in Manchester, after which she returned to the Continent, and the following winter made the acquaintance of another of the Baroness's pupils, destined to be closely identified with the Froebel movement in this country, Madame Michaelis. Madame de Portugall was largely instrumental in introducing Froebelian methods into the infant schools of the Canton of Geneva, where she worked until 1884 when she became head of Madame Schwabe's institution at Naples. She returned to England in 1876 to conduct the first examination of the Froebel Society, and met again not only Madame Michaelis but Fräulein Eleanore Heerwart, whom she must also have known in Manchester.

Miss Barton, finding it difficult to obtain English teachers, was in the habit of sending to Germany when she required staff; among them was Miss Snell who worked in Manchester for forty years and founded a training college for kindergarten teachers in Alexandra Park in 1872. This was known as the Manchester Kindergarten Training College, later the Mather Training College, and among its first lecturers were Mr. W. H. Herford and his daughter Caroline, the founders of Ladybarn School. Mr. Herford was largely instrumental in forming the Manchester Froebel Society in the same year, while his writings include a translation of Froebel's principal work entitled *The Student's Froebel* (1883). In the preface to *The School, an Essay towards Humane Education* (1889), he summed up Froebel's principles and method in two sentences: "The end of education is harmonious development" and "Learn by doing". He added as a piece of advice in the spirit of Froebel: "Never, if you can help it, deprive the child of the sacred right of discovery."

Fräulein Eleanore Heerwart, one of Middendorff's pupils, was in charge of Miss Barton's school from 1861 to 1864. In that year she went to a kindergarten in Belfast and from 1866 to 1874 had a kindergarten and school of her own in Dublin. In 1874 she came to England with the idea of returning to Germany, but was so interested in the possibilities of kindergarten development which she saw in London, that she decided to stay, and accepted a post offered her by the British and Foreign School Society to open a kindergarten training department in connection with their college at Stockwell.

Yet another pioneer was connected with Manchester and London during the 'sixties. Maria Boelte, the daughter of enlightened parents who had given her a good education, had been trained for kindergarten teaching by Luise Froebel at Hamburg. Finding little scope in Germany for her talents, she determined to teach in England, and travelled to Manchester to join Madame Ronge. Madame Ronge sent her to her London school, and she seems also to have worked in some of the Ragged Schools. She recorded that during this period she learnt English in order to help in the kindergarten and school and to train students, and that among the distinguished people who visited the school were Dickens, Mazzini, Charles Kean and his wife. She mentioned also that the Ronges employed an excellent music teacher, Mr. Borschitzky, who realised the importance of giving infants a good musical training.

After the Ronges returned to the Continent, their school was taken over by the Misses Rosalie and Mina Prætorius, who came from Nassau. They conducted the school on progressive lines, but gave up the kindergarten; so Fräulein Boelte obtained a post as a governess with a sister-in-law of Lord Macaulay, who took considerable pains to improve her English. In 1862 she exhibited kindergarten material and work, together with the Misses Prætorius and Heinrich Hoffmann, in the London International Exhibition.

After her pupils had grown too old for her instruction, she came to London and made her home with a well-known physician, Dr. A. Henriques. She gave help and advice in the founding of kindergartens, and in this period of her life met Sir Moses Montefiore, whose son was to do so much for the Froebel movement. She was introduced to the family of Baron Meyer Rothschild, while Sir David Salomon's only daughter was her pupil. She saw the difficulty arising from the lack of trained kindergarten teachers, and the ease with which it was possible to use parts of the apparatus without understanding the spirit behind it.

In 1867 she returned to Germany, and in 1873 emigrated to America, where she married Dr. Kraus, a friend of Froebel's who had settled in America, and with him established the New York Normal Training Kindergarten, where among their pupils was one who was to become one of the greatest American exponents of the kindergarten—Miss Susan Blow.

The 'seventies were years of great educational activity. The first Education Act had been placed on the Statute Book in 1870, and the establishment of *ad hoc* committees known as School Boards, in many places, both paved the way for compulsory education and created bodies with whom it was possible to negotiate.

The Taunton Commission of 1868 had shown weaknesses in the education of middle class boys and girls, and the belief that the German victory in the Franco-Prussian War was largely due to the Prussian schoolmaster, made the country as a whole look with greater favour on educational systems which originated in Germany.

In the sphere of girls' education, the Girls' Public Day

School Company opened their first schools in 1873, offering a cheap and thorough day-school education on the model of the North London Collegiate School, the school which Miss Buss had established in 1850 and of which she was the headmistress.

The College of Preceptors (founded in 1846) appointed Joseph Payne to a lectureship in education in 1871. An ardent disciple of the French educator Jacotot, he believed in the necessity for a theory of education, and was an advocate of the registration of teachers, the extension of secondary education among women and of kindergarten methods. These may have been brought to his notice by the two women members of the Council, Miss Buss and Miss Doreck. The latter had come to England from Württemberg in 1857, and established a kindergarten in Kensington. In 1872 she put forward a scheme, with Miss Buss's assistance, for establishing a training class with lectures for teachers, illustrated by lessons. The Council, after studying the scheme and taking into consideration the good attendance at Payne's lectures in 1871, decided to found a chair of education and to appoint him as the first professor in 1873. In this capacity he lectured on Froebel, and inspired at least two of his hearers, Fanny Franks and Emily Lord, respectively teachers of small children at the North London Collegiate and Notting Hill High Schools, to seek further training in their holidays from Madame de Portugall in Geneva.

Professor Payne also sought further enlightenment abroad, and spent a month in 1874 in investigating kindergartens in Germany, making notes from which the element of criticism was not lacking. Nevertheless, his recorded conclusion was "that there is a substantial value in the exercises of the kindergarten, which pleasurably bring out the active powers of the children —their powers of observation, judgment and invention—and make them at once apt in doing as well as learning".[1]

Professor Payne continued to lecture through the years 1874 and 1875, but his book describing his visits to German schools was not published until after his death in 1876.

The kindergarten movement had become important enough to justify the formation of societies, both for its promotion and to safeguard it from teachers ready to use the name and partially to apply its apparatus without sufficient training or the necessary understanding of its principles. Hence the Manchester Froebel Society (1873) and the London Froebel Society, founded in the following year.

It is interesting to note that the 'seventies were also years of rapid expansion in America; whereas in 1870 there were less than a dozen kindergartens, and all but one conducted by Germans in German, by 1880 there were four hundred scattered over thirty states.

A series of articles by Miss Emily Shirreff in the *Education Journal* had prepared the way for the first meeting of the London Kindergarten Association, which was held at Miss Doreck's house on November 4th, 1874. There were present women who had already played a leading part in the formation of the Girls' Public Day School Company—Mrs. William Grey, Miss Emily Shirreff, Miss Mary Gurney, and others who were to play an equally important part in the new movement— Miss Bishop, Miss Emily Lord, Fräulein Heerwart and Madame Michaelis. The last named was born at Gotha in Thuringia, the daughter of the court physician. In 1863 she heard the Baroness von Marenholtz-Bülow lecture in Berlin, and met, attending the same lectures, Madame

---

[1] *A Visit to German Schools.* Notes of a Professional Tour to inspect some of the Kindergarten, Primary Schools, Public Girls' Schools and Schools for Technical Instruction, pub. 1876.

de Portugall. She became the close friend of the Baroness, and studied under her and Madame de Portugall. Before coming to England, she had taught in Italy and in Switzerland. She came with an introduction to Mrs William Grey, who introduced her to Sir James Kay-Shuttleworth, Miss Mary Gurney and others.

The beginnings of the Froebel Society were informal, through Madame Michaelis and Fräulein Heerwart meeting Miss Bishop, who had been appointed instructress in the kindergarten system to the London School Board, at Miss Doreck's house. They expressed a wish to meet often, and at one of their meetings Miss Bishop introduced her cousin, Miss Manning, who was to become the honorary secretary and treasurer of the new Society. Miss Manning was a friend of Miss Emily Davies, and was one of the founders and benefactors of Girton College. Like her stepmother, the first mistress of Girton, she took a keen interest in the welfare of India. She read a paper on Froebel to the Social Science Congress in 1874.

Miss Doreck, Fräulein Heerwart, Madame Michaelis and the secretary formed a provisional committee, and set about the work of collecting members at a minimum subscription of five shillings. The first members included Miss Buss, who once had said "we shall not have thorough education till we have the kindergarten", Professor Payne, Alfred Bourne, Principal of Stockwell Training College, Madame Froebel, the wife of Froebel's nephew Karl who had settled in Edinburgh, Miss Harriet Jones and Miss Neligan, Headmistresses of Notting Hill and Croydon High Schools respectively.

The Society met frequently; in December 1874 Professor Payne spoke of the greater order in Froebel's system as compared with Pestalozzi's, and in February Fräulein Heerwart opened a discussion on kindergarten literature, mentioning an American magazine, *The*

Kindergarten Messenger, edited by Miss Peabody. Kindergarten literature was for a long time a difficulty, although Miss Shirreff and the Misses Lord did their best to fill the gap; but no one was able to accomplish either the work, or command a public comparable with that of the Americans, Miss Peabody, Mrs. Horace Mann and Henry Barnard, whose compilation *Kindergarten and Child Culture* remains as a mine of information for these early years of the movement.

As an outcome of this discussion, a committee was appointed to translate and adapt some good work on the kindergarten. It consisted of the executive committee with the addition of some others, including Mrs. Berry, a lady who had been very active in forming a kindergarten association in Croydon, and who had secured the services of Madame Michaelis for a kindergarten in the Croydon Public Hall.

The writer is indebted to one of her first pupils for information about this kindergarten. Both boys and girls were between the ages of six and seven, the hours were from 9.30 to 12, and the fee £3 a term. The morning opened with prayers and a formal march round the room. The pupil in question still remembers with great joy the kindergarten games and occupations, particularly "pricking" and "leaping like a frog" round the room after Madame Michaelis who, with her assistants, was as active as any of the children. The reminiscences of one of her contemporaries include "paper folding taught me all the little geometry I ever knew".

By 1875 the Society had taken the title of the "Froebel Society for the Promotion of the Kindergarten System", and had two important projects in hand: lectures for children's nurses, after a scheme for six months' training had been turned down as too elaborate; and the formation of an examination committee of ten members and a President to be elected annually. A preliminary

A Monitorial School, 1839

48]

examination was to be held, by an inspector appointed by the Froebel Society, in reading, writing, arithmetic (including fractions and proportion), English grammar and literature, geography and history. This might be dispensed with by candidates who had passed some recognised examination. The final examination upon which the certificate of the Society was to be given was to include: (1) reading, writing, arithmetic (to decimal fractions), grammar, geography (general and physical), history (English and universal), English literature; (2) Theory of education, history of education, physical education, Froebel's books, geometry, stories, poetry, gymnastics, singing, physiology, physics, elements of zoology, botany and geology, hygiene, kindergarten occupations, and practical lessons given by the students.

The first examination was held in July 1876, the first examiners being Madame de Portugall, Miss Chester, one of the first women elected to the London School Board, and Dr. Frances Hoggan. Among the examinees were Miss Fanny Franks, who obtained a first class, candidates prepared by Fräulein Heerwart at Stockwell, and three from Southampton presented by Miss Sharwood and Miss Sim. Miss Sim had trained under Professor Hoffmann at the Home and Colonial College, and, after having schools of her own at Greenwich and Lewisham, had become Kindergarten Mistress at the Southampton Girls' College. She was to become the first Principal of the Bedford Froebel College.

The Froebel Society sustained the loss of its President in October 1875. Her place was taken by Miss Emily Shirreff, who remained in office until her death in 1897. Miss Shirreff's writings still form some of the most readable books on the subject. They comprised, apart from those she wrote with her sister, Mrs. Grey: *Principles of the Kindergarten System* (1876), *Sketch of Froebel's Life*

(1877), *The Kindergarten at Home* (1882), and a pamphlet, *Moral Training* (1892).

Miss Franks opened her own school, still known as The Camden House School, as soon as she had secured her certificate, and began to train students. Her receptions for all examination candidates continued until the numbers grew too great to be accommodated; they must have proved a pleasant finale to a trying week. At these parties the guests sang kindergarten songs, played kindergarten games and inspected each other's handwork and that of the children in the Camden House School. When her conveniently placed school became the centre for the singing examination, she permitted the examinees to observe the children while waiting their turn for examination.

Among Miss Frank's students was Mrs. Rowland Hill, who became a member of her staff and, when the school moved into Central London in the 'eighties, continued for a time the school in the Camden Road. For many years she gave demonstrations of story-telling, kindergarten songs and games to teachers on Saturday mornings, when children from neighbouring schools came for a "play hour" to St. Martin's Schools in the Charing Cross Road. This course was held under the auspices of the Froebel Society. Later she had her own kindergarten in Enfield.

The Camden House School was one of the first to use Mrs. Curwen's methods of teaching music. This had very close affinities with the Froebel system, and might be said to be, at any rate, partially an outcome of it; indeed, Mrs. Curwen was for some years a member of the Council of the Froebel Society and contributed articles on music teaching to their periodical *Child Life*.

Mr. Ebenezer Cooke, a pioneer in the revolt against South Kensington and a constructive critic of Froebel's methods, taught drawing, painting and nature study to the children and lectured to the students.

Miss Franks's activities were not confined to her own school; her staff and students assisted in the "play hours" which at a later date Mrs. Humphry Ward initiated in a number of schools during the holidays, and at one time they formed a voluntary choir ready to give their services where needed. She interested Mr. Theodore Mander of Wolverhampton in the kindergarten, with the result that he opened a school in the grounds of his own house for his own children and those of his friends, and appointed two of the Camden House trained teachers to run it. At his invitation Miss Franks gave courses of lectures in the week-ends to infant teachers in the town. She was also active in the work of translation. She devoted several years to the translation of Hanschmann's *Life of Froebel*; in order to do so, she went to Blankenburg, where she met old village people who had known Froebel when they were little children; the fresh information she collected was added to the second edition, which she published under the title *The Kindergarten System*.

After Miss Franks retired in 1912, the Camden House School was carried on by Miss Nuth. The present Principal, Miss Betts, moved it from York Place to Gloucester Place. Both Miss Nuth and Miss Betts had trained under Miss Franks and been members of her staff.

Other kindergartens were opened: Fräulein Heerwart opened one in Stockwell in connection with her training department, and in addition she lectured to the students training to become infant school teachers and taking the examination of the Education Department. Most of the schools of the Girls' Public Day School Company had kindergartens, the exceptions being Croydon and Notting Hill, where as long as Madame Michaelis and Miss Lord maintained their schools there was no such necessity; and their preparatory departments were opened only after Madame Michaelis had left Croydon for Kensington and Miss Lord, by that time Mrs. Walter Ward, had founded the Norland Institute. A kindergarten was opened at the Cheltenham Ladies' College in 1876, with twenty-five children and a teacher trained by Madame Michaelis. After 1881, when another of Madame Michaelis's students, Miss Welldon, came to Cheltenham, a properly equipped kindergarten room was provided and the training of students undertaken. A kindergarten in connection with St. Stephen's Church, Cheltenham, was an important element in their training.

Among the early Cheltenham students was a remarkable Indian woman, Pundita Ramabai. She was the daughter of an Indian pundit whose wife was also a scholar, and their daughter had been educated as if she had been a boy. She travelled extensively in Northern India, lecturing and spreading new ideas about the education of women. She was left a widow in 1882, and in 1884 came to England to the Wantage Sisterhood. The sisters arranged that she should study at Cheltenham, and although her studies were not confined to the kindergarten department, she learnt enough to advocate the founding of kindergartens in India in connection with the Ramabai Mukti Mission at Poona, an institution which she started to improve the lot of Indian widows. She lectured to teachers in the Poona schools in 1891, and the news came back to England: "It is encouraging to note that in India Froebel's principles have found an eloquent and enthusiastic exponent in the accomplished and learned Pundita Ramabai."

The Committee of the Froebel Society saw the necessity for training more kindergarten teachers, and for inspecting and registering kindergartens; for it was a very easy matter for teachers who knew nothing of the principles behind the scheme to adopt some of the songs and games, even some of the gifts and occupations, and to call their schools kindergartens. The movement suffered greatly in its early years from these spurious institutions, as it did from teachers who called themselves kindergarten teachers without having passed any examination. In fact, it was necessary at one time to prosecute a man and woman who were issuing certificates upon the receipt of a money payment.

The Froebel Society held regular meetings for its members at which papers were read and discussion invited, and in 1879 a library was established for the use of teachers. In the same year the lectures which the Society had sponsored at the College of Preceptors came to an end, so the committee decided to open a kindergarten and training college in a central position under their own auspices. Miss Bishop was appointed Principal, and her post with the London School Board was taken by Miss Mary Lyschinska. The father of the latter was a Pole who had come to Edinburgh to study medicine, had married an Edinburgh girl and set up in practice there. He had become a well-known figure in Edinburgh, supporting the entry of women into the medical profession and the removal of their general legal disabilities. His daughter had been brought up among the members of the Froebel family, who were also resident in Edinburgh, and she had received her training from Frau Schrader-Breymann in Berlin. She knew Froebel's widow, and translated her reminiscences into English. Her classes under the London School Board were well attended, but so long as payment by results affected the infant schools, no very great progress could be made in method; the infants had to satisfy the examiners! Thus the private kindergarten, and even the private governess, were the means by which the movement spread.

The college and kindergarten were opened at 31, Tavistock Place with ten students to form a nucleus. It ended its separate existence in 1883; the work of training teachers was transferred to the Skinner Street Training

College, as the Maria Grey College was then called, one of the staff, Miss Wallen, being appointed to the staff so that the continuity of the students' training was ensured. Miss Bishop left to establish a kindergarten in Birmingham, and the kindergarten in Tavistock Place was presided over by Miss Esther Lawrence, who later became the second Principal of the Froebel Educational Institute and a pioneer of the cause of nursery schools in London.

The work of inspecting kindergartens and placing them on a graded list was carried out with great care; very definite rules were laid down for the qualifications of inspectors, and directions were given for the points for which they were to look; a method of inspection in which the Froebel Society may be considered a pioneer, for the inspectors of the Education Department at this date seldom, if ever, had had experience of the classroom as teachers.

The movement began to spread by means of kindergarten associations such as had already been formed in Manchester and Croydon. Such an association was formed in Glasgow, where Karl Froebel gave the introductory lecture, and at Bedford, where an influential association appointed Miss Sim to undertake the supervision of a kindergarten for the children of residents in the town, and to train students. The kindergarten was opened in 1882; at first Miss Sim had no assistance in the training of her students, but by the time of her death in 1896, a college of sixty students had been established, while there were one hundred and fifty children in the kindergarten.

Among the students trained at Bedford was Miss Wragge, whose work for the free kindergarten or nursery school will be described later, while the staff at one time included an old student who, as Mrs. Wintringham, became the first British-born woman to enter Parliament. The Froebel College at Bedford has been remarkable for the number of teachers it has sent overseas, often as missionaries, thus helping to spread kindergarten ideas in Africa and Asia.

Under Miss Sim's successor, Miss Walmsley, a second kindergarten was added, a hostel for students opened in 1899, and for a few years the College gave a domestic science training in connection with Gloucester Training College in addition to the kindergarten training. This was very much in accordance with the ideas prevalent at the Pestalozzi-Froebel House, Berlin, which aimed at training girls for home-life in all its aspects.

In common with other teachers' associations, the Froebel Society hoped much from the appointment of Mr. A. J. Mundella to the Vice-Presidency of the Education Department in 1880, for he had the reputation of being an enlightened administrator; and Froebelians were always conscious of the fact that they had a mission to all the children of the country, not only to those whose parents were prepared to pay fees for their education. He had already shown his interest in the training at Stockwell College by presiding over a meeting in which the students were given their certificates, and upon one occasion, near the end of his term of office, he announced in public that he owed his interest and knowledge of the kindergarten to Miss Emily Shirreff, the President of the Froebel Society.

In June 1880 a letter came from Mr. Herford urging the co-operation of the Froebel Society with the Manchester Kindergarten Association in sending a deputation to Mr. Mundella, asking for the introduction of Froebel's system into the government elementary schools. It was agreed that a joint deputation, with Miss Shirreff at its head, should "urge that Her Majesty's Inspectors be directed to allow as teaching suitable to the age of the children under seven, that which is known as kindergarten training, and to employ in the examination of the infants in any properly constituted kindergarten, a method of ascertaining results approved by capable exponents of the system". As a result, the Code of 1881 showed some modifications in that infant schools were required, in order to qualify for the merit grant, to include "simple lessons on objects and the phenomena of nature and common life" and appropriate and varied occupations. In an accompanying circular, a specific reference was made to Froebel's principles. "The Code assumes that besides suitable instruction in these elements (reading, writing and arithmetic) and in needlework and singing, a good infants' school should provide a regular course in simple conversational lessons on objects and on the facts of natural history, and a proper variety of physical exercises and interesting employments. . . . It should be borne in mind that it is of little service to adopt the gifts and mechanical occupations of the kindergarten unless they are so used as to furnish real training in accuracy of hand and eye, in intelligence and obedience."

The Froebel Society concerned itself with discussions as to the best way it could help teachers to take advantage of the Code; assistance which was badly needed as there is ample evidence that many teachers regarded "kindergarten" as a subject on the time-table rather than principles which should permeate the whole curriculum.

Among the members of the deputation in 1880 was Mr. Alfred Bourne, Superintendent of the three metropolitan colleges of the British and Foreign School Society, who had been instrumental in appointing Fräulein Heerwart to Stockwell Training College and establishing a model kindergarten at Stockwell. It was largely due to his energy that the kindergarten section in the International Health Exhibition held in London in

A School-room in 1870

1884 was a success. Children were seen at work and play, those of Miss Frank's kindergarten amongst them. They went on unconcernedly with their occupation in spite of the crowds surrounding their enclosure.

At a conference held at the same time, Miss Manning and Fräulein Heerwart read papers. Miss Manning's paper was entitled "What Froebel did for Young Children"; in the course of it she said: "The teaching is not direct instruction. It trains the senses and the observing powers through handling and doing; it exercises the muscles and limbs, it takes advantage of the imitative faculty, it appeals to the fancy by means of stories and talks, it works through the affections, it draws forth helpfulness and self-respect. The kindergarten ought to be open for the instruction of young girls, nurses and nursemaids, where they might learn how to treat and how to train the children, to young mothers and to all who have charge of little children."

Mr. Alfred Bourne spoke on the Code in relation to infant schools. In the course of his remarks he said that the number of children under six in elementary schools had increased by 36 per cent. in ten years: that school life was short in England, only 12 per cent. of the scholars being over twelve and only 4½ per cent. over thirteen. "All depended on the use of their first years. There were two rival theories in the field; one party said 'take time by the forelock, teach infants their prescribed tasks before they are legally required to repeat them; by mere reiteration the tasks will become familiar'; the other party said 'develop the infant's powers; teach him to attend, to construct, and "chance" the standards. When his powers and observation have been trained and his interest excited, he will find no difficulty in the three R's.' The Code of 1884, with its complementary instruction to inspectors, went far to satisfy the requirements of infant teachers; the difficulty was not the Code but the expense.

This was the gist of the matter. A kindergarten required small classes, each with an intelligent and sympathetic teacher. These cost money, and to provide the necessary funds, Froebelians must instruct and elevate public opinion.''

In the course of the discussion, Mr. Herford of Manchester remarked that there was a good deal of playing at kindergarten in government schools but very little live kindergarten. "The introduction of a box of cottons, sticks and blunted needles to be played with once or twice a week was a hollow sham.''

Mr. Mundella remained in office in the Education Department for five years, and his interest in education and in the kindergarten continued and had far-reaching results.

The Froebel Society took the opportunity given by the Cross Commission to present a series of resolutions drawn up in the first instance by Mr. Bourne and Miss Lyschinska, and presented by Mr. Bourne and the Hon. Mrs. Buxton to the Commissioners in 1886. Among other points, they asked that care should be taken in building schools; that ample space be allowed for games and exercises; that stress should be laid on the use of manual occupations and on suitable toys for children of five years old in accordance with the instructions of the Code; that no examination in reading should be held for children under Standard I, and that boys in infant schools who did not take needlework should be allowed to take drawing or another manual occupation as an alternative; that infant school teachers preparing for the government certificate should be set a special paper to test candidates' knowledge in the principles and methods of infant education, and that inspectors of infant schools should understand Froebelian methods.

The Cross Commissioners took little interest in infant education, but the Code of 1892 gave recognition to the

Froebel certificate as a qualification for an assistant mistress-ship. Infants were no longer to be examined in the three R's; it would be considered satisfactory if children over seven could pass the examination in Standard I. This was accompanied by Circular 322 on "the Instruction of Infants", which stated that two leading principles should be regarded as a sound basis for the education of early childhood: (1) The recognition of the child's spontaneous activity and the stimulation of this activity in certain well-defined directions by the teachers; (2) the harmonious and complete development of the whole of a child's faculties. The teacher should pay special regard to the type of movement which can alone secure healthy physical conditions, to the observant use of the organs of sense, especially those of sight and touch, and to that eager desire for questioning which intelligent children exhibit. All these should be developed simultaneously, so that each stage of development may be complete in itself.

The circular continued: "It has been strongly urged that sufficient attention has not been paid in the past to these principles; indeed, it is often found that kindergarten occupations are treated as mere toys or amusing pastimes, because they are attractive for children, and the intellectual character of the 'gifts' of Froebel is disregarded, whereas the main object of these lessons is to stimulate intelligent individual effort. You should direct the attention of teachers to the chief consideration which underlies true methods of infant teaching, viz. the association of one lesson with another through some one leading idea or ideas. On the other hand, you should caution teachers against the mere repetition of the same exercises and lessons, the progressive character of the whole scheme of instruction should be constantly kept in view, and each exercise should lead up to something beyond itself."

A list of varied occupations was appended, and was obviously drawn from Froebelian sources.

The London School Board, which ever since 1874 had shown an interest in kindergarten methods, passed a resolution in 1896 that assistant teachers in infant schools must obtain a kindergarten certificate before being eligible for increase of salary; at the same time the School Management Committee appointed a special sub-committee to advise on the best mode of improving method and curriculum in the infant schools. Their report contained the following sentence: "The witnesses who have given evidence before us are unanimous in declaring that the methods and results of infant school work have greatly improved during the last twenty years and that the improvement is due to the influence of the kindergarten."

During the 'eighties other kindergartens training students were founded, among them Miss James's at Stamford Hill; and the Froebel Society started a journal. The early numbers showed an interest in the American free kindergarten; recorded the opening of the first kindergarten in Portugal in 1852, and contained a letter from Fräulein Heerwart on the difficulty of translating Froebel's writings from German to English and explaining that a too literal translation was no help. It was during this decade that Froebel's chief works became available in English, although his letters were not translated until 1891 and the *Pedagogics of the Kindergarten* only in 1893.

In 1882 the Society held a celebration for the centenary of Froebel's birth, and Fräulein Heerwart represented it at the Conference held in Dresden. British Froebelians were at all times conscious of belonging to an international movement, and welcomed fellow Froebelians from all over the world. They were particularly alive to the movement in Germany and America.

In 1883 Fräulein Heerwart decided to return to Germany, where she continued to teach until 1902, when she retired to Eisenach which she made a centre for a world-wide association of kindergarten teachers until her death in 1911. The following passage occurred in her obituary notice in *Child Life*, the organ of the Froebel Society: "It was largely due to the influence and advocacy of Fräulein Heerwart, while head of the kindergarten department at Stockwell College from 1874 to 1883, that Froebel's educational theories won acceptance in England and the kindergarten became an essential part of English education."

In addition to her work at Stockwell and on the Executive Committee of the Froebel Society, she had inspected kindergartens; served as an examiner for the practical examination; edited, written and translated by way of propaganda; and compiled a collection of songs suitable for English children.

When she retired, the British and Foreign School Society decided to give up the training of private students as kindergarten teachers, although the kindergarten was continued as an independent school by the Misses Crombie. The society continued to interest itself in enlightened methods of infant teaching, and opened in 1884 a college and school at Saffron Walden with that end in view.

These years saw also the development of the examination, which tended at first to be overloaded with practical and academic subjects, with the result that very few students completed the course. In 1884 it was decided to hold two examinations and to issue two certificates. The Lower Certificate was intended for assistant kindergarten teachers and governesses; the Higher Certificate, which could be taken in two parts, for those who wished to take full charge of kindergartens. The syllabuses of these examinations are interesting because they show what was considered essential for the right conduct of a kindergarten, mainly Nature Study, Mathematics, Music and a thorough knowledge of the Occupations. The syllabus of the Lower Certificate consisted of:

1. The biographies of Pestalozzi and Froebel illustrating their works and teaching.

2. (i) The Principles of Education as taught by Pestalozzi and Froebel; (ii) Their application to the teaching of elementary subjects.

3. General knowledge of familiar plants and animals and the ordinary phenomena of nature. Questions also to be asked on the care of animals, plants, etc.

4. Practical knowledge of the occupations. Viva-voce candidates would be expected to show a general knowledge of the kindergarten gifts and occupations, and to have worked out three special occupations to be announced by the Council two years previously.

5. Music. To sing, in time and tune, songs connected with the games, and to answer elementary questions on time, keys and intervals.

For the practical examination in teaching candidates were required:

1. To tell a story.

2. To conduct a game.

3. To give a lesson on one of the occupations (choice of occupation to be left to the candidate).

4. To give a lesson on an elementary school subject.

5. To conduct some simple gymnastic exercises.

Part I of the Higher Certificate included Geometry, Algebra, Physiology, Physics, Botany, Natural History (from which a pass in the same subject in a Senior Local Examination would exempt a candidate), Music and Singing, a practical knowledge of the Occupations, the History of Education with special reference to Pestalozzi and Froebel.

Part II was entirely a professional examination, and

consisted of papers on Theory of Education, Practice of Education and Hygiene.

The practical examination consisted of ability to (1) tell a story, (2) conduct a game, (3) show notes of a lesson on each of the following subjects: (a) one of the occupations, (b) one of the elementary school subjects, (c) one of the elementary science subjects, (4) conduct some gymnastic exercises.

Optional papers could be taken in drawing and in German.

After a time the Lower Certificate came to be known as the Elementary Certificate, and existed in a somewhat modified form until 1917. In 1889 a Preliminary Certificate to serve as some criterion of general education was added: for among the reasons for the somewhat slow development of the kindergarten were the small number of students coming forward for training and the low educational standard of some who did apply.

With regard to the practical examinations, great importance was attached to the correct handling of the gifts and their manipulation, while Froebel's singing games formed a link between his followers and their pupils.

For long there was a strong feeling that there was a difference between the children's free play and the games organised by their teachers. This attitude was justified on the score that many children had not sufficient imagination to organise their own play, and that play to be of educational value had to have certain characteristics. A good kindergarten game should afford an opportunity for intellectual training, ethical teaching, physical exercise, dramatic action, musical and rhythmical training and concise, simple and accurate language. The games Froebel himself invented were given pride of place, but teachers and students were encouraged to invent new games, and gradually the traditional English nursery rhymes found their way into the kindergarten, although traditional games were still frowned upon as being often unintelligible to children and over-emphasising sex. Miss E. R. Murray of the Maria Grey College, writing in *Child Life* in 1901, quoted Froebel: "The freer and more spontaneous the arrangements, the more excellent is the effect of the game. Encourage your little ones to be always observing and then to think over what they have observed, for this alone promotes genuinely original action." In the more critical atmosphere of the twentieth century she wrote that the acceptable games were (*a*) nature games (*b*) trade games, and that the nature games led to close observation of nature. She felt that the value of school games lay first in their social training and as a part of that training the cultivation of originality and freedom of expression; and secondly in bodily exercise and activity; and added for the benefit of those still adhering rigidly to the letter of Froebel's teaching: "It is a poor compliment to a reformer to turn his methods into iron bands to stop the progress of free thought."

Froebel's *Mutter und Kose-Lieder* was translated in 1886 by the Misses F. and E. Lord, and his singing games and finger plays found their way into English kindergartens, in spite of the fact that they spoke of an environment which was foreign to British children. A year after their publication, one of the most faithful friends of the move-ment, Mr. H. Courthope Bowen, wrote *"Mutter und Kose-Lieder* was collected and composed and organised some fifty years ago, for little German children—mainly those who were surrounded with country sights and sounds and occupations. For little English children you will require something different—you will require what is English or has become English. All of physical nature, of the country that you can actually bring into the cities, that you can place within sight and touch of the children,

use freely. For the rest, draw upon the children's homes
and from the life by which they are surrounded. To do
otherwise is to break at once with Froebelianism. For
these little city children we should not tell of 'The Fish in
the Brook' but of the 'Sparrow in the Street'; not of the
'Nest with its Birdlings' but of the 'Cat and her Kittens',
etc." The situation became even more ridiculous when
these songs and games were carried overseas to Australia
and New Zealand, although in justice to the pioneers in
this country it should be mentioned that Mrs. Berry had
translated some of the Mother Songs as early as 1876, and
that she had visited the Baroness von Marenholtz-
Bülow in Dresden and found that she agreed that "The
songs and games must represent objects familiar to the
children in their own country".

The publication of the Mother Songs led to a flood of
children's songs and games, some suitable, others reach-
ing an absurdity to which Professor Graham Wallas
called attention in his famous criticism of the system.
The ditty he quoted was probably never used in a
kindergarten inspected by the Froebel Society:

> *"We are but little toddlekins,*
> *And can't do much, we know,*
> *But still we think we must be nice,*
> *For people love us so."*

The fact that it was possible for any unauthorised
person to introduce some of the gifts and occupations,
say pricking, mat plaiting and sticklaying, and a few
singing games, and call the school a kindergarten, was a
tiresome handicap; and the need for fully trained and
certificated teachers was paramount.

In this connection it was important that there should
be one, not several, examining bodies, and the Froebel
Society welcomed an invitation from the Manchester

Kindergarten Association suggesting an amalgamation
for examination purposes. After a great deal of preliminary discussion, a joint board was formed in 1887 and held
its first examinations in 1888. In deference to the wishes
of the Manchester Association, the number of subjects was
drastically cut; the Elementary Examination consisted
of three papers in which one was devoted to Natural
Science; the practical part of the examination remained
the same, except that candidates who failed the singing
but passed in the theoretical part of the music examination might obtain their certificates with the addition of
the words "except in singing, wherein the candidate
failed to satisfy the examiners". Drawing from Nature
was the only optional subject.

In 1886 the Bedford Kindergarten Company joined
the Board, and in 1893 the Home and Colonial Society,
which had been training and examining kindergarten
students since 1856. The Joint Board was fortunate in
having the same chairman for twenty-one years, Mr. H.
Courthope Bowen, the Headmaster of the Grocers'
Company School, Hackney Downs.

It is convenient here to trace the subsequent history of
the National Froebel Union, as the Joint Board came to
be called. The Manchester Kindergarten Association
seceded in 1889 and soon ceased to exist, but the Mather
College, as the Manchester Kindergarten Training
College came to be called, continued to present candidates for examination until 1925. As time went on, the
number of candidates began to increase; by 1890 the
examinations were held in twelve centres, including
Ireland, and in 1892 there came requests for examination centres from India, Australia, Cape Colony and
Canada. A difficulty arose through these requests—that
of finding persons capable of carrying out satisfactorily
the practical examinations.

It was decided in 1898, in the case of Cape Colony,

that the written papers could be taken overseas and a written statement given that the candidate had passed. This could be supplemented by the trainer's testimonial as to practice. The certificate could be completed if a suitable opportunity presented itself. In 1905 a Kindergarten Union was founded in South Australia for the purpose of promoting kindergarten principles, the establishment of free kindergartens and the training of teachers, and in 1907 the National Froebel Union found it possible to form an examination centre in New Zealand. In 1910 an Indian Committee proposed granting their own certificate; they were advised to consult certain Froebelians holding important positions in India, and this certificate came into being. Its holders, on coming to England, were permitted to take the Teacher's Certificate of the National Froebel Union after one year's further study.[1]

In 1898 the period of training for the Higher Certificate was raised from two to two and a half years, and in 1904 the National Froebel Union became incorporated and obtained a new constitution in accordance with a scheme made by the Board of Education.

The syllabus itself had undergone many changes. Drawing had at one time consisted of presenting for examination a volume of chequered paper with intricate designs evolved by putting various units together in certain regular orderly ways. This was compulsory; blackboard drawing from nature formed an optional course.

Mr. Ebenezer Cooke, a pupil of Ruskin's and a friend of Ablett's, undertook the examination in blackboard drawing in 1889. He had himself experimented in teaching art in kindergartens since 1878, notably Miss Frank's kindergarten. He was instrumental in introducing colour,

---

[1] With the abolition of Certificate B all candidates from abroad preparing for the English Froebel Teacher's Certificate now come to Great Britain for training, except for those in Kenya who take Certificate A.

which he contended children demanded, in the form of brushwork, and considered that they should try to copy nature, not patterns laid down for them by their teachers. This method became popular during the next ten years, but it was not until 1893 that chalk and colour work appeared in the list of "occupations" appointed for examination by the National Froebel Union.

After his first experience as an examiner, he attacked by a written protest the type of drawing presented by the examination candidates as "neither natural nor Froebelian".

As a result, the regulations for drawing were altered in 1890 to drawing done on sheets of brown paper pinned on the blackboard and done quickly as in class, simple in treatment, similar to the best drawings of children and the best early art. Watercolour drawings were to be done with the brush under similar conditions. In 1895 Miss Penstone, who represented the Home and Colonial Society on the Board, protested that Froebel drawing (i.e. the geometrical designs in squares) was trying to the eyesight, and in 1897 it was resolved that it should no longer be a compulsory subject. In 1904 the section called Gifts and Occupations was renamed Gifts and Educational Handwork, and for reasons which will be given at length farther down, in 1906 the gifts were dropped from the syllabus and a wide choice of educational handwork was permitted in their place.

In 1905 the preliminary examination no longer admitted to the N.F.U. Higher Certificate, and a School Certificate from one of the Universities was required. This was important because one of the reasons for the Board of Education's refusal of recognition was that the entry requirements were lower than those required for the government certificate. A letter from the Headmistresses' Association the same year asked the joint Board to consider altering their examination in such a way as to make it possible for the holders of the Higher

Certificate to undertake lower form teaching. A committee was appointed to meet the Headmistresses' Association, and as a result the requirements for the certificate were considerably stiffened in order that its holders might be able to teach children up to twelve. Papers in literature and geography were added, and methods of teaching arithmetic and reading included in the paper on Organisation and Method. Two examiners were to be present at the practical examination.

In 1910 the Secretary of the Froebel Society wrote to the National Froebel Union requesting that Froebel's Principles should be made compulsory and received the following reply: "That in the opinion of this Board, the revised syllabuses for the certificates of the National Froebel Union, though they have the effect of somewhat diminishing the stress that has hitherto been laid upon the letter of Froebel's writings, are yet in complete accord with the spirit which animated Froebel's work, whilst at the same time they embody some of the ascertained results of recent educational thought and practice."

The examinations for the Elementary Certificate were held for the last time in 1917, and the Higher or Teacher's Certificate became the accepted qualification.

In 1915 Miss Esther Lawrence, the Principal of the Froebel Educational Institute, put forward a scheme for internal examination. She considered that the existing examination system gave too little scope for research and expansion to the training colleges, and was not always a true test of a student's capacity. It is interesting to note that a very similar suggestion had been made by Professor Findlay of Manchester in 1896, and in spite of the fact that both Madame Michaelis and Miss Franks had been in favour of it, it had been turned down on the plea that it would have borne hardly on the kindergartens preparing a few students for the examination, and that it would be difficult to get a uniform standard.

By 1915 the National Froebel Union was not looking with favour on the private kindergartens preparing students for examination, and was ready to make special arrangements for internal examination in the by now well-established training colleges; consequently a committee was set up to consider the matter, and in 1918 met the principals of the training colleges concerned. It was decided that a Joint Examining Body should consist of three members of the National Froebel Union's Committee, three members of each college staff and the Board of Education Assessor. The subjects of the internal examination were to be the same as for the National Froebel Union's external examination, and syllabuses and draft papers were to be submitted to the National Froebel Union. Scripts were to be marked first by the college lecturers and then sent to the National Froebel Union. The college marks for handwork and practical teaching were to be submitted, and not less than 25 per cent. of the candidates were to be examined.

These changes had been preceded earlier in the year by a deputation to the Board of Education to ask for recognition for the Higher Certificate. The Froebel Educational Institute had already been inspected by the Board of Education, and told that the certificate could not be recognised so long as the examination remained an external one. It was therefore no surprise when the representatives of the Board made it clear that they would not accept such an examination as an alternative to the Teacher's Certificate, and emphasised their view that the courses of training and not the mere possession of a certificate were the primary consideration.

Mr. Roscoe, the Secretary of the Royal Society of Teachers, wrote pointing out the desirability of making the training a three years' course for purposes of registration, and Miss Esther Lawrence, the Principal of the Froebel Educational Institute, Miss Walmsley, the

Principal of the Bedford Froebel College and Miss Murray, Vice-Principal of the Maria Grey College, met to make the necessary arrangements. The three colleges, which were the first to gain internal status and the recognition of their certificates by the Board of Education, adopted this course in 1922, and two years later the external examination was extended to three years. During the next eight years three other colleges asked for internal recognition: St. Mary's College, Lancaster Gate, in 1927, the Rachel McMillan College in 1929 and Clapham High School in 1930.

St. Mary's College was a Church of England college which had had a department for training kindergarten students since the beginning of the century. During the principalship of Miss Helena Powell many students trained with the intention of becoming missionaries overseas. The history of the Rachel McMillan College is related below; the Clapham High School Froebel department dates from 1898, when it was established by Mrs. Woodhouse. The head of the department was for some years Miss Lilian James, who annually presided over the Froebel Society's Summer School. This department has developed into a separate college, the Philippa Fawcett, under the auspices and control of the London County Council.

In 1927 the governors of the National Froebel Union assumed a responsibility for the training as well as the examining of candidates, whether they sat for the internal or external examination, by making arrangements for inspecting and registering colleges and training departments. The first inspector and educational adviser was Mr. Thomas Raymont.

Two certificates were issued on the results of the Teacher's Certificate Examination, Certificate A to those candidates who presented themselves from "approved institutions", Certificate B to those whose training had been undertaken in uninspected and unregistered colleges and schools or by private study.

Meanwhile the National Froebel Union had extended its work in other directions. It was felt that some additional qualification was necessary for those who wished to train students, and in February 1914 the Trainer's Diploma was instituted. Suggestions were made at the same time for a Handwork Diploma, but the First World War prevented this scheme from taking shape until 1920.

The National Froebel Union celebrated its Jubilee as an examining body in 1937 with a reception at County Hall. In 1938 it was reunited with its parent body, the Froebel Society, to form the National Froebel Foundation, under the directorship of Miss R. L. Monkhouse, with premises in Manchester Square.

The years which followed saw a decrease in the number of external students but, on the other hand, an increase in the number of certificated teachers, who in many centres asked for lectures and added the Froebel Certificate to their qualifications. Certificated teachers and graduates of British universities are permitted to take the Froebel Teacher's Certificate in one year if they attend a Froebel training college, or in two years if they attend recognised part-time classes. In 1931 the National Froebel Union decided to grant its Certificate A only to those who had had a full-time course in a Froebel training college and qualified teachers who had attended recognised part-time classes, and to recognise no more schools training only for Part I.

This decision was fortunate, for with the alteration in the status of teachers in 1945, all holders of Certificate A became eligible for recognition as "qualified" teachers. Certificate B will in a year or two cease to be awarded.

The publication of the McNair Report on the Train-

A Class of Infants using a Froebel Gift, 1906

ing of Teachers, and the subsequent formation of
Institutes of Education in most British universities, has
led to a close connection between the National Froebel
Foundation and the universities of London and Birmingham.

In London, students from the Froebel Educational
Institute, the Maria Grey and the Rachel McMillan
Training Colleges are able to enjoy many of the amenities of university life, and to receive at the end of their
training, if they are successful, the Teacher's Certificate
of the London Institute of Education in addition to the
National Froebel Foundation Certificate. The students
of Westhill Training College, Selly Oak, have been
granted the same privilege by the University of Birmingham.

The history of the National Froebel Union has indicated that Froebelians were alive to the fact that Froebel
had spent his life labouring for the harmonious development of the whole nature of man from infancy to manhood, and that to its founder the kindergarten was never
an end in itself but an entrance to a vast and harmonious
edifice. Consequently they were alive to the possibility
of developing further some of the conceptions of education to which the kindergarten had given rise.

Modern music teaching owes a great deal to Mrs.
Curwen's adaptation of Froebel's principles to this purpose, and the kindergarten band, which was one of the
earliest features of the kindergarten, has developed into
the percussion bands of the present day, while the singing
game has given place to free musical movement under
Dalcroze, Ann Driver and others.

The impetus to take handwork, other than the needlework traditional in the education of girls, beyond the
confines of the kindergarten and its transition classes
came from Sweden. Uno Cygnaeus, a Finnish educator
who had known Froebel and who was regarded as the

father of the primary school in Finland, had seen the desirability of teaching peasants some form of domestic industry in which they could employ themselves during the long winter evenings and thus supplement their incomes from farming. He developed a system which could be taught in school, and which might be carried on in the home after school days were over. The government of Finland made this part of the rural school curriculum in 1866. Cygnaeus regarded it as a logical extension of the activity principle of the kindergarten. The work was imitated and adapted by another disciple of Froebel's, Otto Salomon of Sweden, who was well acquainted with the dictum that man only understands thoroughly what he is able to produce. He worked out a system of woodwork suitable for children from ten to fourteen years of age, and established a training college at Nääs which attracted observers from all over the world. This form of woodwork was known as Slöjd and found its way to England: among those who visited Nääs were Miss E. Lord and four of her students. A Slöjd Association was formed in England with which the Froebel Society had very friendly relations, although they refused to amalgamate the two societies in 1889. Otto Salomon's book *The Theory of Educational Slöjd* was published by Messrs. Philip & Son in 1893, and the idea of hand and eye training by graded woodwork became popular in the last decade of the century, leading to the introduction of other forms of handwork in schools for older children. It may be said that it was due to the Slöjd Association of Great Britain and Ireland that manual training received definite recognition in the upper standards.

The Froebel Society was also closely allied with the Child Study Association, with which it for a time shared premises. This society owed a good deal to American inspiration, particularly to the work of Dr. Stanley Hall of Johns Hopkins University, who had formed parents' associations to obtain records of parents' personal observations of their children.

In England, the aim of interesting parents and of giving some training to children's nurses had not been forgotten, and the 1890s saw the beginnings of two interesting institutions with this end in view.

Miss Lord, who had been training students in Notting Hill, had come across a number of girls who had a genuine love and understanding of little children, but not sufficient mental ability to pass the examinations for kindergarten teachers. She hoped to found a new profession for women, and at the same time to render a service in the true spirit of Froebel to young children who often were left to ignorant women during their most impressionable years. After her marriage to Mr. Walter Ward she was able to put her plans into operation. She continued for a time the Norland Place kindergarten, but gave up the training of students; instead she persuaded Madame Michaelis to leave Croydon and come to Norland Place with fifteen students. These students practised and observed in the Norland Place kindergarten and at a crèche and kindergarten which had been opened in Chiswick.

Mrs. Ward outlined her plans for training children's nurses in a series of drawing-room meetings, the first of which was arranged for her by Miss Jones, the Headmistress of Notting Hill High School; several headmistresses, including Miss Buss, were present. The college was to be called "The Norland Institute for the Training of Ladies as Children's Nurses for Young Children", and had for its objects: (a) supplying the public with ladies as trained nurses for their children; (b) forming a new occupation for young women whose circumstances do not enable them to undergo the long course of professional training now essential to a success-

ful educational career, even where they are endowed
with sufficiently good intellectual abilities.

The first plan allowed for nine months' training, three
months in the Institute, three months in hospital and
three months' probation in some institution for children
or in a family. The course of instruction was to comprise
needlework, hygiene and useful knowledge (this
included making beef-tea, the preparation of poultices
and first-aid); diet, how to make simple puddings,
porridge, etc.; Froebelian instruction and hospital
training.

The Norland Institute opened in September 1892 with
four probationers; they spent their first three months
in the Institute under the supervision of Miss Isabel
Sharman, who had been one of Mrs. Ward's students,
and taken a first-class Froebel Certificate in 1886.
During these months they had to learn, as far as possible
in so short a time, all that would be useful to them in a
nursery. Three hours daily was devoted to intellectual
work; nature lessons were given regularly twice a week
all through the term; stories suitable for children were
discussed and the art of relating them was practised.
Singing was taught twice a week, and kindergarten songs
and games were learnt and practised. Some of the
simpler kindergarten occupations were worked through,
and the place they should take in the amusement and
training of the child was carefully explained.

In addition to lectures on simple hygiene, the probationers saw demonstrations of cooking suitable for
young children, while laundry work and needlework
were not neglected.

Then there followed three months in hospital.

Mrs. Ward had to meet with a considerable amount of
opposition; the educational world accused her of giving
a superficial kindergarten training, the hospitals were
afraid of admitting probationers for three months. How-

ever, these difficulties were overcome, and by 1904 Mrs. Ward had opened model nurseries in Pembridge Square, where she had moved the Institute in 1900. By 1919 the training took fifteen months, and in 1932 it was placed under a Board of Directors.

The nurses went out wearing a distinctive dress, and were encouraged to keep in close touch with the Institute. Employers had to consent to three stipulations. The nurses (*a*) should not be required to take their meals with the servants, (*b*) should not be required to scrub floors, (*c*) should not be asked to polish grates or carry coals.

The Norland Institute continues to-day, in its post-war home at Chislehurst, the work of training children's nurses, who continue to find work in homes, and have found a new sphere as superintendents of nurseries under the Ministry of Health after obtaining the Certificate of the National Nursery Examination Board.

The Norland Institute led the way, which has been followed by other bodies, so that the college-trained children's nurse has won her way to professional status and is no longer looked upon with surprise and suspicion, and the Norland nurse has played her part, as the founder intended, in the ever-growing attention to child welfare.

In the last decade of the nineteenth century the majority of upper- and middle-class children received their first lessons in their own homes, and in 1895 a club was opened with the object of interesting parents in new methods of education and of assisting them in the bringing up of their children.

The Sesame Club, which is to-day a purely social club, was opened with the intention of forming a rallying-point for all societies which were trying to help forward the reform of education, and it was hoped that it would become a recognised rendezvous for persons interested in education in all its branches, whether as professional teachers or as parents. The premises included a classroom for lectures and debates. Mr. Montifiore and three other members of the Froebel Society were on the committee, and the society undertook to hold readings of Pestalozzi's *How Gertrude Teaches Her Children* on Wednesday evenings. Classes were arranged for the children of members, which could be watched by members who applied to the secretary the day before. These included courses on drawing and handwork from Mr. Cooke, a class in Slöjd to teach children the elements of carpentry, and a course for members of the club and their friends on nature study. It was the intention to publish Sesame Club papers once a month on a subject of educational interest. The first of these was a paper by Lady Isabel Margesson, a connection by marriage of Miss Emily Shirreff, on "The Froebel System". In it she described suitable lessons for children from three to six drawn from the gifts, drawing, singing and story-telling, and emphasised the importance of "connection" in story, games and occupation. Her interest had first been aroused by teaching her own child of three. On other occasions, Mrs. Walter Ward advocated the value of manual work, and Madame Michaelis came and spoke about the plans and scope of the Froebel Institute. Mrs. Curwen gave a paper on methods of teaching music, and a paper was given on teaching arithmetic through Froebel's gifts.

The Sesame Club provided a platform for various forms of progressive education, and amongst others for Miss Charlotte Mason, the founder of the Parents' National Educational Union. She protested that she did not represent "New Education" but was trying to help parents and governesses in conducting their own schoolrooms. Though she had shown in her book *Home Education* that she had studied the kindergarten and had seen Fräulein

Heerwart at work, her methods differed very considerably from those of the Froebelians. She was of the opinion that for the Froebel method a teacher of superior intelligence was needed, but "put a commonplace woman in charge of such a school and the charmingly devised gifts and games and occupations become so many instruments of 'wooden' teaching". She did not think it possible nor necessary that every nursery should become an organised kindergarten, for she was of the opinion that much of the sense training could be better obtained by the ordinary occupations of a well-regulated home. Her system does, however, pay a great deal of attention to accurate observation and to nature study.

By 1899 the Sesame Club had nine hundred members, but there were associated with it people who were interested in its educational aims but did not want to belong to a social club; they formed the Sesame League, and resolved to open a house for Home Life Training on the lines of the Pestalozzi-Froebel Haus in Berlin, and persuaded Fräulein Schepel, who had worked with Frau Schrader-Breymann for many years, to come over from Berlin to become its first Principal.

Sesame House was opened in Hampstead in 1899, and by the third year of its existence had sixty-five students, among them two from Finland and four Parsees. The course included the care of children, nature study, and work in the flower and vegetable garden, household management, cooking and the right use of foods. Both a fee-paying and a free kindergarten were attached to the institution. A close co-operation existed between Sesame House and Edgbaston Training College, where Miss Bishop was carrying out the same ideas. Three students were exchanged with three from Birmingham, that the London students might have some experience of teaching older children and the Birmingham students experience with the children of the poor. The domestic work of the college was undertaken by five of the students.

But the most important undertaking of the eventful last ten years of the century was the founding of the Froebel Educational Institute. Mrs. Salis Schwabe had for some time wanted to see established in England an institution as wide in its implications and as far-reaching in its influence as the institute she had founded in Naples. She wished it to be established in London, to consist of a training college for training teachers on Froebelian lines, a school for children up to the age of fourteen, which should aim "at that development of character and faculty from within which is a fundamental part of Froebel's teaching, as well as the organised evolution of the child's whole nature and its creative expression in productive work, and a free kindergarten on the same principles for the children of the poor".

She worked very hard to obtain the necessary funds, and it is recorded that she saved £2,000 by her own economies, which included putting down her carriage and travelling on the railway, third class. She persuaded Sir William Mather, who was interested in infant and nursery schools in Manchester, to become the first chairman, and Mr. Claude Montefiore to become honorary treasurer. A meeting was held at the Westminster Palace Hotel on October 25th, 1892, when a council was formed with instructions to raise money and find premises for this new project, and two years later Mr. and Mrs. Leopold Rothschild lent their house in Hamilton Place, Piccadilly, for a meeting of subscribers, at which most of the prominent Froebelians spoke, as well as Mr. Kekewich of the Education Department.

The Empress Frederick, on her frequent visits to England, took a keen interest in the enterprise. She had for long interested herself in the kindergarten and had

A Classroom in 1952

been instrumental in providing Frau Luise Froebel with a pension.

The foundation-stone of the new college was laid in 1893; the first lectures were given in temporary buildings in 1894, and a year later the Froebel Educational Institute was opened at 45, Colet Gardens, West Kensington. Madame Michaelis was asked to become Principal, and the college opened with the sixty-six students she brought with her from Norland Place. Mrs. Salis Schwabe did not long survive this successful beginning, for she died in May 1896 at Naples. Her ambition to add a kindergarten for poor children was not forgotten, and from 1899 to 1918 the Institute provided a school in Challoner Street, West Kensington. Madame Michaelis, who had given the greater part of her life to furthering Froebel's principles in England, retired in 1901 and died in 1904. She was President of the Froebel Society after Miss Shirreff's death in 1897 until 1900, when she was succeeded by Mrs. Walter Ward. Her successor at the Froebel Educational Institute was Miss Esther Lawrence, who had worked with her for seven years, five as Headmistress of the school, and two as Mistress of Method in the college. Under her the interest in the free kindergarten or nursery school was further developed, the Notting Hill Nursery School opened with the support of the Michaelis Guild in 1908, and two years later another nursery school was opened in Somers Town.

The Michaelis Guild was the name given to the Old Students' Association; the members made social work, more especially social work among children, a very important part of their activities. Many members learnt to transcribe braille in order that blind children might be kept supplied with books.

Mr. Claude Montefiore, as treasurer and chairman, continued to take a great interest in the Institute, as he did in the Froebel Society, and in 1921 he succeeded in transferring it to its present home, Grove House, Roehampton Lane, where a spacious house and grounds made expansion in many directions possible. The school remained at Colet Gardens until the Second World War. After a period of evacuation, it returned to a home near the college at Ibstock Place.

It is not possible to write of the Froebel Educational Institute without mentioning Miss R. Lulham, whose development of the teaching of nature study had a wide influence far beyond the confines of the college. Froebel himself had emphasised the importance of observing nature, and the National Froebel Union was the first examination body in this country to examine in nature study. A great deal of importance in the early days was attached to the kindergarten really having a garden, but in some ways American teachers were ahead of English. The English teacher was too ready to think she had interested children in nature when she had brought tadpoles, or a plant or even a few twigs into the classroom, while the American teacher was more ready to take her pupils out of doors to natural surroundings. The increasing interest in natural science in both countries led to the observation of nature in the kindergarten and junior classes being appreciated as a sound foundation for more advanced work and an impetus for carrying these studies into later school life. In 1903 a Nature Study Exhibition was held in London sponsored by one of the newspapers. The same year, through the enthusiasm of the Rev. Claude Hinscliff, Miss Lulham, Miss von Wyss of the London Day Training College and others, the School Nature Study Union was formed. This has ever since kept alive the study of nature in both schools and training colleges. The Froebel Society showed its interest in and encouragement of the new society by allowing its members to borrow books from the nature study section of its library.

The free kindergarten had become a very important side of American philanthropy, and many Americans expressed surprise to find that the idea was not taken up to any great extent in England. The reason is to be found in the difference between American and British Education Acts. In America, education is a matter for each state; in some states, education was not compulsory until the twentieth century. Where it was compulsory, the statutory age was usually six or seven, not five, as was and is the case in England since 1880. Consequently where free kindergartens existed in Great Britain, they tended to be for children below the age of five; and after a Royal Commission had reported on the education of children of pre-school age in 1905, they were known as nursery schools. Nevertheless, Sir William Mather had established a free kindergarten in Salford for children from two to six or seven years of age in 1871. It was built on the site of a cleared slum, and provided baths, meals, training, rest and play. Its first superintendent had been trained in Berlin. In 1900 a free kindergarten was opened at Woolwich by Miss Adelaide Wragge. Miss Wragge had been trained at Bedford by Miss Sim, and she had established at Blackheath a training college and kindergarten, and by continued study in America and elsewhere became through her school a real exponent of Froebel's philosophy. The Blackheath Kindergarten Students' Union founded the Hoxton Mission Kindergarten mainly for children whose mothers were at work all day. They undertook late evening visits when the parents might be expected to be at home, and established for them a savings bank opened one night a week after 8 p.m.

The free kindergartens in connection with Sesame House and the Froebel Institute have been already mentioned, and in connection with the latter, St. James's House in Notting Dale, kindergarten rooms were rented from the St. James's House Day Nursery, and the children were allowed the use of the garden where they had a sand-pit. They were encouraged to sing, work and play out of doors as well as indoors, and parents' meetings were held in the evenings. Another free kindergarten of about the same date was opened in Canongate, Edinburgh (1903). Here again the garden and a sand-pit were important features. The children were from three to five years of age, they were supplied with pinafores and given their own special pegs upon which to keep them. Some other features of the modern nursery school appear here. The children were encouraged to keep pets, chiefly doves and rabbits, and to attend to them themselves. They helped to set their own meals and were encouraged to help in other domestic occupations.

The Vacation Schools for London children, initiated in the early years of the century by Mrs. Humphry Ward at the settlement which now bears her name, had a kindergarten with a sand-pit for the youngest children.

In 1904 a People's Kindergarten was opened in Birmingham by Julia Lloyd, who had previously spent a year at the Pestalozzi-Froebel Haus; the name of this school was changed to Nursery School in 1917.

But the names most closely associated with the development of the nursery school, and the recognition by both the government and the public of its obligations to the pre-school child, are those of Rachel and Margaret McMillan. These two sisters, who combined an American and Scottish upbringing, approached the problem from the point of view of the child's physical well-being. Margaret McMillan was elected to the Bradford School Board in 1894, where she agitated for school baths and medical inspection, and was instrumental in introducing a scheme for feeding school children. Rachel McMillan qualified as a sanitary inspector, and became a travelling teacher of hygiene under the Kent County Council.

The sisters joined forces in London, and in 1908

opened a treatment clinic in Bow. After two years this was closed and instead a school clinic was opened in Deptford and a camp school set up in the garden. Their care for the children's health and training in personal hygiene led a year later to an open-air nursery school for children under five, with a trained teacher and a girl helper. In 1914 the London County Council granted the use of a site, and here children were cared for, fed and taught during the First World War. Rachel McMillan planned and organised while Margaret undertook propaganda for the cause of nursery schools.

The provision of nursery schools was included in the Education Act of 1918, but reluctantly dropped by Mr. Fisher when the call for economy came in 1921. The movement found, however, champions in the House of Commons in the persons of Lady Astor and Mrs. Wintringham, and a strong ally among permanent officials in Sir George Newman, the chief Medical Officer of the Board of Education.

A Nursery School Association was formed in 1923 with Margaret McMillan as its first President, and Miss Grace Owen, Principal of the Mather Training College, Manchester, where a special training department for nursery school teachers had been opened in 1917, was the first honorary secretary.

The efforts of this association were directed towards persuading local authorities to open nursery schools and nursery classes, which were encouraged by the President of the Board of Education after 1924. The Froebel Society assisted in a campaign during the L.C.C. elections of 1928 by paying for the printing of a pamphlet entitled "A Plea for the Under Fives".

By the end of 1933 there were fifty-nine recognised nursery schools in England, thirty-two maintained by local authorities and twenty-seven by voluntary committees. In this connection there should be mentioned the nurseries established in distressed areas by the "Save the Children Fund".

Many persons interested in the training of young children deplored the change of school at five and wanted to maintain the same environment until the age of seven. The Bradford Education Committee succeeded in amalgamating nursery and infant schools successfully.

The training of nursery school teachers was undertaken at the Rachel McMillan Training College, founded by Margaret McMillan in memory of her sister who had died in 1917. From 1917 the college gave a year's course, recognised for grants by the Board of Education, to certificated teachers, and also gave a three years' training to students wishing to specialise in nursery school work. Through the generosity of Lady Astor funds were raised for a college building, and the Rachel McMillan Training College was opened by Queen Mary in 1930. Margaret McMillan died the following year, but the nursery school at Deptford has to a great extent served as a model for nursery schools elsewhere.

With the growth of the movement, other colleges made provision for training specifically for nursery schools. The National Froebel Union examined for a Nursery School Diploma between 1932 and 1939, after which provision was made in the ordinary Teacher's Certificate for examining candidates trained for nursery school work.

The Second World War led to the establishment of war-time nurseries under the Ministry of Health; the best of these approximated to the standards of nursery schools, and they made the public much more conscious of the existence and value of such schools. Since the war the demand has far exceeded the supply. In large towns the housing shortage had led to an increase in the number of flats, and the difficulty of obtaining domestic labour has led to the development of private fee-paying nursery schools. In all nursery schools the children's health, diet and habits are of supreme importance, and all owe something to those first free kindergartens in Manchester, London, Edinburgh and Birmingham.

Important developments in the attitude of progressive Froebelians towards Froebel's teaching, with consequent changes in the schools, took place both in America and in England during the twenty years between the last decade of the nineteenth century and the outbreak of the First World War. These were all as Froebel himself would have wished, in the direction of greater freedom for both teacher and child, and were the result of greater understanding of the child's mental and physical well-being.

The Child Study Associations on both sides of the Atlantic have already been mentioned, while a scientific age gave increasing attention to the physical and psychological needs of childhood. Froebelians had always had to meet a certain amount of criticism. Of these one of the most interesting because of the eminence of the critic was that of Professor Graham Wallas, who said that Froebel's work was necessarily conditioned by the thought of his time; that as a pre-Darwinian evolutionist he taught that the development of the individual and the species proceeded from within, and that outside circumstances had no influence except as providing a favourable or an unfavourable environment; and that this belief was likely to produce just the educational exaggerations which were to be found in him and his followers. He then proceeded to enumerate these faults, some of which were a minimising of human tradition and contrivance as a formative influence, the neglect of the training of attention, and, through attention, habits and character. Froebelians were apt to ignore the distinction between work, and play as the relief after work; they postponed to an unnecessarily late period the acquisition of such arts as reading and writing. The misunderstanding of the whole conditions under which men gain knowledge, and the unnecessarily long postponement of the introduction of a child to the highest standard of human achievement —real music, real literature, real art, etc.—were serious faults. Other faults were characteristic of his time; he exaggerated and simplified the distinction between the stages of a child's development, he sentimentalised, he wrote extremely bad verse and his followers wrote worse; he was a symbolist. The result of this would naturally be that intellectual and material softness of which secondary teachers who received pupils from the orthodox kindergartens complained.

This lecture was received with a good deal of indignation, but there must have been an element of truth in the criticisms, and in any case the movement was soon to rid itself of the symbolism and the neglect of the arts. The accusation that the kindergarten tended to softness and sentimentalism and prolonged unduly the state of childhood tends to reappear with every educational reform, an accusation which can only be combated by an investigation of the results when the pupils have reached maturity.

Progressive Froebelians in America and in England were by the end of the century reframing their methods in the spirit of the master, but with regard to modern discoveries in psychology and science. An English specialist, Dr. Hughlings Jackson, was the first to discover that the fine nerves and muscles develop latest, and this was taken up by Dr. Stanley Hall and other American leaders of the Child Study movement. They condemned pricking and sewing, pea and stick work, the threading of small beads, all work indeed that involved delicate manipulation with the fingers. The eyes likewise were to be safeguarded from fine and exact paper folding and drawing with a pencil on lines, these were to be replaced

Physical Education in 1906

by brushwork and free drawing. Free play, in which the children took the lead and the teacher was in the background, took the place of the organised kindergarten games; while songs and refrains with a good swinging rhythm, each containing some interesting idea related to the child's own life and lending itself to dramatic action, took the place of the "Mother Songs" in fostering among the children unity of feeling and interest.

The pragmatic philosophy, which Stanley Hall, William James and others were making popular in the United States, had its educational implications, and progressive Froebelians were quick to see how Froebel's teaching with its emphasis upon activity, observation and natural development corresponded with this fresh teaching. Its greatest exponent was Professor Dewey of Chicago, who worked out in his demonstration school a scheme based upon the children's interests and share in the life of the community. He had able lieutenants in Colonel Francis Parker and Miss Patty Smith Hill.

The break away from what had hitherto been thought of as the orthodox kindergarten led to a long controversy waged fiercely on both sides. The chief exponent of the older methods was Miss Susan Blow, who attacked not only the socialised Dewey school but the free play which Professor Stanley Hall and his child study groups had initiated, and also the concentric programme which was popular in some quarters. This was the practice, which found favour in England as well as in America, of entering all school activities for a week or sometimes longer, round a single topic, usually one associated with nature study. Miss Blow argued with truth that this led to a neglect of literature, and indeed in the hand of the less-skilled teacher, the story, music and poetry introduced might be of a very inferior quality provided they "fitted" and the activities which followed might become desperately boring to the children. "That d——d chicken again" is an apocryphal story belonging to this period.

The socialised Dewey school, the result of Professor Dewey's work at Chicago and based upon his teaching, became widely known throughout the civilised world. He worked out a scheme based on Froebel's philosophy of self-activity and unity extended through the junior school, or as these classes are termed in America, "the Grades". He believed that the first aim of the kindergarten teacher should be to create a community. He believed with Froebel that a child lives in his play and that the benefit he receives from it lies: "(1) in his so taking hold of a subject that he seems to have originated it, and (2) in having it suggest to him other things, so that he in his own individual way works out a teacher's ideas and thus gets the benefit of the experience of others." He retained the four building gifts to be used as ordinary blocks were used—as media to illustrate different phases of the work, when they could be adapted absolutely to the work, not the work laid out in order to bring in the gifts. With them he used larger blocks which he thought more suitable for group work, and when desirable he added other material and toys. As the children grew older, he introduced them to other ideas associated with the world around them, such as the farm and the house. Their handwork, simple carpentry, weaving and pottery was associated with the interest they were pursuing. One of his chief American exponents, Miss Patty Smith Hill, has expressed the aims of the socialised school as follows: "The mutual rights of the individual and of the society demand that society realise its obligation to educate every child. . . . The protection and development of society, however, demand that the process by which the child is educated bring to his consciousness an ever-deepening sense of his obligation to social service."

Professor Dewey's writings became well known throughout Europe, and at a later date he was called in as educational adviser in countries as wide apart as Turkey, Japan and the U.S.S.R.

The changes which were taking place in America became known in England at the turn of the century through the work of Miss M. E. Findlay, who had spent three years in the United States studying first under Professor Stanley Hall, but for most of the time at Chicago under Professor Dewey and as a member of the staff of the Francis Parker School. Upon her return to England in 1898, she joined the staff of the Froebel Educational Institute, where she remained until her death in 1912.

Her educational outlook is perhaps best summed up in a quotation from her writings: "The most characteristic feature in the life of the young child that renders it capable of training is 'activity'."

She found an enthusiastic co-worker in Miss E. R. Murray of the Maria Grey Training College, who began in 1901 to make dolls'-houses with the little children and to do weaving with the older children in her kindergarten, and the following year opened a discussion at the Froebel Society on "Symmetrical Paper Folding a Waste of Time".

The cleavage between the old and new interpretation of Froebel's teaching did not assume the proportions it had in the United States, and the change to the newer and freer methods of interpretation was welcomed by the majority of kindergartens within a comparatively short time, while the gradual emancipation from gifts, occupations and set drawing in favour of educational handwork in the syllabus of the National Froebel Union brought relief to those training to become kindergarten teachers, and gave scope to those of them who had artistic gifts.

It was as well that Froebelians had modernised their

methods before they had to meet the challenge of the
Montessorians. Dr. Montessori first visited this country
in 1912, and the Froebel Society was prepared to welcome her; but it soon became clear that she did not wish
to be associated with them nor was she prepared to admit
that her methods had any connection with the teaching
of Froebel. She caught the imagination and attracted
the attention of the public in a way the Froebelians had
never done. This was partly due to the changed attitude
towards the child which the kindergarten and modern
scientific knowledge had brought about, partly to the
great increase in interest in education and partly to the
power of the Press.

Kindergartners were distressed to see the introduction
of graded sense apparatus, which they felt might become
as stereotyped as the gifts and occupations they had
abandoned, and they disapproved strongly of Dr.
Montessori's attitude towards imaginative myths and
fairy stories. On the other hand, the publicity she enjoyed undoubtedly called attention to the importance of
education in its early stages, and from this Froebelians
benefited.

The controversy is an old one now, and it can be safely
stated that the schools benefited from adopting the small
chairs and tables which children could move easily for
themselves, and that teachers learnt to combine with
the group work of the Froebel-Dewey School, the greater
attention to the individuality of each child insisted on by
Dr. Montessori, and the knowledge that in sense training
and in acquiring some skills children could be left to
make their own individual progress.

The Froebel Society continued its work; in 1916 the
title was changed to the Froebel Society and Junior
Schools' Association, and the number of branch associations carried the work through the country, arranging
lectures for teachers, parents and students. In 1918 there

were branches at Bradford, Bristol, Cambridge, Derby, Hull, Leeds, Leicester, Northamptonshire, Northumberland, Durham and the North Riding, Norwich, Rotherham, Sheffield, Stafford and Calcutta; while the annual summer school was well attended. In 1921 the London Society was hearing a lecture on mental tests and arranging an exhibition of individual occupations, while the summer school was taking notice of the possibilities of script writing.

The Council joined in a deputation to Mr. Fisher, the then President of the Board of Education in 1922, to protest at the use of untrained teachers in infant schools as an economy measure. In 1924 Professor Patty Smith Hill visited England, and in a letter to the Froebel Society wrote: "When the Council broke away from the literal, and preached the liberal interpretation of Froebelian views, they had rendered a great service to education." In 1929 the Froebel Society joined with the New Education Fellowship, the Nursery School Association, and the Montessori Society in a conference with American teachers, under her leadership.

The efforts to interest parents in the health and school work of their children have been outlined above, but it was not until 1929 that a separate Home and School Council was formed, to which the Parents' Associations of schools for all ages and of every kind could be affiliated.

The years between the wars saw a great development in the study of child psychology both in Europe and America; this had its influence in the schools in a greater attention to the individual needs of children and a deeper understanding of the age at which they might be expected to acquire such skills as reading and writing.

In America in particular experiments were being tried with the curriculum. Dr. Kilpatrick, a follower of Professor Dewey, and other progressive teachers, particularly the staff of the Francis Parker School, had experimented with giving greater freedom to their pupils in the choice of interests which they projected into as many fields of knowledge as possible; reserving time for those essential skills which were necessary for the child's adjustment to his environment. "The Project", as it came to be called, found favour in a great many English schools, and led to the child centred activity programmes of the present day. This sometimes has been carried rather far and has led on both sides of the Atlantic to a belief that it is as well if sometimes the school is "teacher centred". Professor Décroly worked out a somewhat similar system in some of the Belgian schools, centring his work about the four fundamental needs of man: food, shelter, protection and work. These he regarded as the fundamental interests as well as the fundamental needs.

Perhaps enough has been written to show that there is a very direct connection between the work and ideas of Froebel more than a hundred years ago and the modern or progressive attitude towards children and their education; and that the debt of all who have any love or understanding of children and their needs to Froebel and his followers is incalculable.

CHAPTER III

FROEBEL AND THE ENGLISH PRIMARY SCHOOL OF TODAY

DESCRIPTION OF PRIMARY SCHOOLS

PROFESSOR W. H. KILPATRICK of Teachers' College, Columbia University, used to assert to his educational philosophy class that "with Froebel, education took a right-about face". This was a large claim, especially coming as it did from one who was no indoctrinated kindergartner. A century has elapsed since Froebel's revolutionary movement made its first impact on English education as a result of the pioneer work of Madame Ronge and others about the year 1854. The story of their work and the avenues through which its influence penetrated into the various branches of English education is told in Chapter II, and there also it can be seen how subsequent students and teachers of early childhood, building on to the Froebelian tradition, modifying, developing and discarding, have brought into being the pattern of education so familiar to us today—and not only familiar, but with all its contributory threads so closely interwoven that it is with difficulty and with hesitation that we attempt to trace the distinctively Froebelian contribution through the hundred years which lie immediately behind us.

No student of Froebel can fail to recognise and appreciate the essential mainspring of his doctrine—his love, reverence and (in the light of the available knowledge of his time) his understanding of childhood. The term "child-centred" is modern, but the conception which it embodies can be traced back to Froebel; and this is the master-key which has led to a pattern of education, not

95

only of the youngest children but throughout the formative years of childhood and youth.

It does not appear that the first Froebelians in this
country were much, if at all, concerned with the type of
schooling provided for the masses of the people. As with
so many other innovations, early kindergarten schools
and classes were private ventures, sponsored by individuals or voluntary bodies, and their influence penetrated
only gradually into the state system of education. The
study of this permeation may therefore well begin with
an attempt to re-create a picture of schooling provided in
this country for the young children of the masses at the
time when Madame Ronge was lecturing on the kindergarten system and demonstrating it in her Infant Garden
at Hampstead.

Infant schools were already well established, and
served the double purpose, principally in industrial
areas, of minding young children whose mothers were at
work and of giving instruction in the elements of reading,
writing and arithmetic. In addition to the infant schools,
there were the dame schools, where no doubt the function of minding took precedence over that of instruction.
It is probably a mistake to paint too grim a picture of
these early infant schools, for while the buildings were
dreary, the furniture rigid and the methods formal, it
should be remembered that Robert Owen had not been
unaware of the value of play in the open air, of bodily
exercise and of the importance of the formation of good
habits. Pestalozzi's belief in the use of objects and pictures in teaching young children had been disseminated
through the work of the Rev. Charles Mayo and his
sister. There is, moreover, a good deal of contemporary
evidence to show that a kindly and benevolent attitude
was often, if not usually, adopted towards pupils of ten-
der years. Froebel's "right-about face" therefore was not
from cruelty to kindness or from ignorance to knowledge

—it was a change in attitude towards childhood. Froebel saw in the child and in his life and activity something of infinite value and (to him) sacred. His view was in complete contrast to the contemporary idea of child nature as something to be repressed; it was to be encouraged, fostered, developed. Knowledge and skill were not regarded by Froebel as something alien and remote from child nature, to be imposed on a mind whose only function was receptivity. We may not accept the Froebelian doctrine of innate ideas, but our infant schools today testify to our belief in childish activity as an essential part of the learning process.

Accounts of the first kindergartens to be opened in England [1] stress certain features which are of great interest in comparison with our best ideals of education in primary infant schools today. In these early kindergartens opportunity was provided for children to play in a garden. For a typical group of not more than twenty-five children to a teacher, two "spacious" rooms were provided—one with appropriately sized tables and chairs for seated occupations, the other with clear space for games and having direct access to the garden.

The children attended for comparatively short hours, usually mornings only, taking some of their occupations to be continued at home, thus providing a link between parents and teachers.

There was an elaborate outfit of specially designed educative material (gifts and occupations) by means of which the children learned in a school not based on books.

Great stress was laid on the culture and training of the teachers.

No doubt, to pass from one of these early kindergartens to a contemporary infant school would have been to experience existence in two entirely different worlds—

[1] Ronge, *The English Kindergarten.*

worlds that had hardly anything at all in common. But to bridge the intervening century, and to look into our modern infant schools with some of Froebel's fundamental principles in mind, may afford a means of estimating the extent of his influence today.

School buildings provide the approaching visitor with his first clue to the theory of the purpose of the education for which they were designed. Not a few of our school buildings in use today were standing before the year of Froebel's death. Many others speak to us of 1870, the introduction of compulsory schooling and the attempt in urban areas to combine solidarity of structure with maximum capacity in minimum space. The old "three decker" school, so familiar in many cities, was built with these objects in view. The pattern of the central hall with class rooms leading out of it reminds us of standards of staffing in days when the head teacher from her desk in the school hall could keep all her staff—some of them pupil teachers and monitors—under constant and vigilant supervision. In the infant schools, though the galleries have mostly been removed, traces of them can still be seen, recalling the closely packed rows of infants immobilised except for their eyes and fingers for the greater part of the day.

Village schools of the same period give no cause for complacency either. Set, as they often are, with the country surging up to their very doors, the schools were obviously built by their pious founders with one eye on the ecclesiastical origin of the foundation and the other on the elimination of any influences likely to distract the attention of the young pupils from the task in hand.

Perhaps this brief survey of these ancient buildings may serve to emphasise the gap that existed between the Froebelian ideal in the matter of the educational setting and the provision for the rank and file of English children which was at that time considered not only adequate but

generous—that so many of these buildings remain sub-
stantially unchanged must not be taken to indicate complete lack of progress. In fact, the teacher who has so far
in this record been conspicuous by absence must now
make an appearance. Whatever has been done to modify
the austerity—indeed, to lend a touch of grace to these
old buildings—has been almost entirely the unaided work
of the teachers. Little gardens have been made along the
side of the playgrounds, trees have been planted (and
have flourished and even borne fruit!), shrubs in pots,
rabbits in hutches, birds in cages or cotes bear witness
to teachers' passionate belief in the young child's need
for contact with growing and living things. The word
"unaided" was used above, but a tribute must be paid to
the enthusiasm which has inspired children to contribute,
in paper bags, the soil for their gardens. Could faith
and devotion go further? Stimulated and encouraged by
the enthusiasm of the teachers, some progressive local
authorities have provided sand piles and paddling pools
in infant school playgrounds. School architects still tend
to demolish all trees and shrubs on a new site so as to
reduce it to a dead level, although in this matter also
there are signs of progress, as may be seen when the more
recent buildings come under review.

School building, to meet the needs of an increasing
child population, health demands and changes in school
organisation, was in full swing at the outbreak of World
War II (1939). Although the buildings of that date
showed, in many respects, an advance on the earlier
ones, there was still very little obvious sign that the
needs of young children were being recognised and
catered for. Such progress as was made in regard to easy
access to playgrounds (still *not* as a rule gardens), number and siting of toilet provision, arrangements for serving meals and for storing toys and beds, was due almost
entirely to the unflagging work of the nursery school

teachers and their association. Many voluntary nursery schools in buildings of light and even ramshackle construction were, and still are, shining examples of how little children can thrive and grow more happily in such an environment than against a rigid background of glass, tiles and chromium. Froebel would have taken these schools to his heart, and indeed, many of the teachers reveal, at the lightest scratch, their Froebelian origin and loyalty. Still another fashion of school architecture is now making its appearance. Where a light and adaptable structure is employed, and where there is a readiness to break away from traditional types of building, the interests of young children are most likely to be well served. The introduction of colour and gaiety is also warmly welcome. But buildings cost money, and at the time of writing problems of materials, labour and sites are more than formidable. Teachers of young children often regret the over-elaboration, as it seems to them, of some school buildings, and feel that they could carry out their work no less effectively in a school that came nearer to Margaret McMillan's ideal of "a shelter in a garden".

To move now from the building to what goes on inside it, perhaps the first consideration is that of the organisation and planning of the school. The kindergarten ideal of not more than twenty-five children to a teacher suggests the belief that children need space in which to grow and that the unique personality of each child must be intimately known by the teacher. Moreover, the kindergarten has never aimed at a rigid classification either by age or ability, preferring a somewhat mixed group in which children learn from each other as well as from the teacher, as they do in a good-sized family.

The infant school has never reached this ideal (if ideal it be) partly because the numbers allocated to one teacher are always too large and partly because learning is thought of more exclusively in terms of school skills (chiefly the three R's) than in terms of social behaviour and the acquisition of skills other than the three R's. There have been experiments in what has been called "family classification", i.e. forming each class of children of varying age and ability, but they have usually been abandoned for the above reasons. The notable exception to this is the small country school, where of necessity one teacher has a group with an age range covering the whole infant stage of 5 to 7 plus years combined with an equal or even greater range in ability. This organisation is tolerated as long as the numbers are small, but if they rise, for example, into the thirties the burden is felt to be too great.

The present shortage of teachers, combined with the increased war-time birth-rate, has not only delayed the reduction in the size of classes but has unfortunately had the reverse effect. The educational world at large has not yet outgrown the bad old belief that young children are easier to teach than older ones, and that because they are small they need less space. There is, moreover, at present a tendency to classify by ability (of a clearly defined and somewhat narrow type), and to make school skills, especially reading, the criterion of progress. All this is far removed from the Froebelian ideal of the essential value of every child without reference to his intellectual ability, and a disinclination to isolate intellectual from practical and social abilities or to set supreme value upon it. It would seem true to say, therefore, that in the matter of classification the primary schools have been and are hardly, if at all, affected by Froebelian influence; nor does the present trend seem to be in a Froebelian direction.

In the days of the first kindergartens there would not appear to have been very much difference between them and the infant schools as regards the planning of the

daily programme as distinct from the material, or subjects, of which the programme was composed. The
planning of any programme reflects, more or less, the
current beliefs regarding the way in which children
learn. A hundred years ago the specialised psychology of
young children was still a closed book, and school work
was planned chiefly on the assumption that learning was
mainly a receptive process and that teaching should be
administered to young children in small doses of brief
duration. Froebel was the prophet of the active nature of
the learning process, but it was not until much later that
psychologists showed that active learning could not be
confined to brief twenty-minute or half-hour periods.

A comparison therefore of the daily programme of a
kindergarten with that of an infant school of from about
1854 to within the last twenty-five or thirty years shows
little difference in time allocation, apart from the longer
day of the infant school.

This can be seen from a study of the programmes here
appended.

Both programmes show a series of brief periods, some
as short as ten minutes, none longer than thirty with
some attempt at alternation between the more and the
less active "subjects". (The two programmes A and B are
inserted by kind permission of the Principal of Stockwell
Training College.)

In the case of programme A, the kindergarten re-
assembled in the afternoon, but this practice was by no
means general. It will be noticed that the entire programme is devoted to traditionally Froebelian occupations, and that while hymn singing appears daily, there
is no other form of religious instruction. This, in all
probability, reflects the Froebelian belief that the mother
fulfils this most important function in the child's life, and,
moreover, that the whole of the child's education is, in
fact, religious. It is probably not too much to claim that

PROGRAMME A

Kindergarten   *Stockwell College, 1878*

Morning

	Monday	Tuesday	Wednesday	Thursday	Friday
9.15	Hymn and Poetry	Hymn and Singing	Hymn and Poetry	Hymn and Singing	Hymn and Poetry
9.45			Registers marked and closed		
10.0	Building	Stick laying	Planes of Wood	Building	Stick laying
10.40			Free Play		
10.50			Gymnastic Games		
11.25	Sewing	Pricking Beadwork	Mat plaiting	Sewing	Pricking Beadwork

Afternoon

	Monday	Tuesday	Wednesday	Thursday	Friday
2.0			Registers marked and closed		
2.15			Gymnastic Games		
2.45	Mat plaiting	Paper folding	Sewing Modelling	Paper folding	Mat plaiting Games
3.30	Words of songs	Natural History	Story	Natural History	
4.0			Hymn and Dismissal		

103

PROGRAMME B

Stockwell College Infants' Practising School, 1878

	9–9.10	9.10–9.30	9.30–10	10–10.15	10.15–11	11–11.10	11.10–11.25	11.25–12	2–2.15	2.15–3.15	3.15–3.30	3.30–4	4–4.15
MONDAY	Repeating Words of School Songs	(1) School opened with Singing and Prayer (2) Registers marked	(1) Repeating Scripture (Pupil Teachers) (2) Registers closed.	Change and Physical Exercise	Writing on Slates (Pupil Teachers)	Spelling on Blackboard	Recreation in Playground	Number (1) Mental (2) on Blackboard and Slates	Registers marked and closed.	Kindergarten occupations (Students and Pupil Teachers)	Change and Physical Exercise	Spelling (Students)	(1) School closed with Singing and Prayer (2) Dressing.
TUESDAY	Ditto	Ditto	Scripture Lessons. Old Test. (Mistress and Pupil Teachers)	Ditto	Number (1) Mental (2) on Blackboard	Ditto	Kindergarten Games	Reading	Ditto	Dictation (Boys) Needlework (Girls)	Ditto	Reading (Students)	Ditto

Day													
Wednesday	Ditto	Singing	Ditto	Writing (Boys) Needlework (Girls)	Ditto	Gallery Lessons (Pupil Teachers)	Recreation in Playground	Ditto	Reading	Ditto	Scripture Lessons New Test. (Mistress and Pupil Teachers)	Ditto	Ditto
Thursday	Ditto	Reading	Ditto	Dictation (Boys) Needlework (Girls)	Ditto	Gallery Lessons (Students)	Kindergarten Games	Ditto	Number	Ditto	Scripture Lessons (Pupil Teachers)	Ditto	Ditto
Friday	Ditto	Marching and Kindergarten Games	Ditto	Reading	Ditto	Gallery Lessons (Students)	Recreation in Playground	Ditto	Ditto	Ditto	Scripture Lessons (Mistress and Pupil Teachers)	Ditto	Ditto

A Second-year Student acts as Mistress on Wednesdays

most of the early kindergartners were consciously aware of the spiritual significance of all their undertakings.

In programme B scripture lessons and the three R's make their appearance. It is noted in the records of Stockwell College that a "transition" class was introduced to bridge the gulf that existed between the procedure of the kindergarten and that of the infant school.

The gallery lessons referred to are those toward which H.M. Inspector of Schools, the Rev. M. Mitchell, levelled such enlightened criticism (see Chapter II). There may still be seen in some infant schools the glass-fronted cupboards in which were kept the "objects"— stuffed birds and smaller mammals, lumps of mineral matter and samples of manufacturing processes—which formed the subject-matter of these lessons. To the modern mind they may seem incredibly dull fare for little folk; but the writer can testify from remembered experience to the thrill of expectation, the charm of odd fragments of information and the exquisite joy of being allowed to handle the precious object. Today everything is put into children's hands. No doubt there is gain in physical and intellectual freedom, but is there possibly some loss, the loss of regard for what is in some sense precious and remote? We are today too close to this problem to be able to give a cool and unbiased judgment; it is one of the problems recognised in the present day and passed on to future generations for solution.

It is interesting to note that gallery lessons were entrusted to students and pupil teachers. This was no doubt because the lessons were self-contained and could be prepared (and criticised) as units complete in themselves. In the course of the lesson the student could exploit her own dramatic powers, and by keeping the children on the *qui vive* could avoid the worst disciplinary pitfalls.

There is always a time-lag between theory and practice, but it is now a well-established custom in most infant schools, as in modern kindergartens, to organise the day in relatively large blocks of time within which children have freedom to follow one pursuit or to change it according to the demands of the particular situation. The relation of these blocks of time to the pursuits which they control will be dealt with presently.

PROGRAMME C

Infant School Programme, 1952

Daily Programme, 5–6 years (Reception)

9	Assembly	Hymn, Prayer, Greetings, Birthdays.
9.10	Play Out of Doors	Sand-pit. Water Play. Jungle Gym., Slide, Tricycles, Big Toys, Balls, Ropes, Hoops, Boxes, Ladders, etc.
10	Play Out of Doors and Indoors	Materials for "Home and Street". Kitchen (baking and washing), Bedroom, Bathroom (dolls), Building Blocks, Shop, etc. Introducing Picture Books (reading) in Book Shop.
10.40	Break	
11	Number	Games. Floor Games with Bean Bags, Quoits, Skittles, etc.
11.30	Literature or Music	Stories, Poetry, Drama, or Music and Movement, Singing or Percussion Band.
12	Dinner Preparation	
1.30	Materials for Arts and Crafts or Walk (once a week)	Clay, Wood, Cardboard, Paper, Fabrics, Paints, Pastels, Coloured Paper, Large Crayons.
2.15	Break	
2.30	Play Occupations	} Jigsaws, Beads (manufactured). "Seat and Table" Material.
3.10– 3.30	Religious Instruction	

20 minutes break A.M.
15 minutes break P.M.

PROGRAMME D

Infant School Programme, 1952

Daily Programme, 6–7 years

9	Assembly	Hymn, Prayer, Greetings, Birthdays.
	Play Indoors and Outdoors	Materials of "Home and Street" for Kitchen, Bedroom, Bathroom (dolls), Building Blocks, Shops, Hospitals, etc.
10	Out of Doors (P.E.)	Skipping-ropes, Hoops, Balls and Bats, etc.
	Reading	Reading Material and Books.
	Writing	Children's individual Books for pictorial and written story, diary, etc.
	Break	
11	Number	Scoring Games.
		Shops for Weight, Measurement and Capacity.
12	Literature or	Stories, Poetry, Drama or
	Music	Singing, Music and Movement, or Percussion Band.
1.30	Materials for Arts and Crafts or	Clay, Wood, Cardboard, Paper, Fabrics, etc.
		Paints, Pastels, Crayons, Coloured Paper, etc.
	Walk (if fine)	Visit to Gardens, Wood, Quarry, Railway or Building of Houses, Schools, etc.
2.15	Break	
2.30	Play Occupations or Walk Record	Jigsaws, etc. (seat and table).
		Picture or Writing.
	Outdoor Games (P.E.)	Balls, Ropes, Hoops, etc.
3.30	Religious Instruction	

Programmes C and D are in current use in a large infant school, and are inserted by the courtesy of the Director of Education for the City of Leeds. They explain themselves, and will be familiar in form and content to most present-day readers. The selection of playthings from which children choose their occupations has been widened to include most experiences of present-day childhood. The inclusion of dinner preparation shows that the school day is an unbroken whole for most children and many teachers. In programme D it can be clearly seen how learning of the basic skills (three R's) is largely an integral part of the play which has been developing in content and complexity during the years from 5 to 7 plus.

PROGRAMME E

Daily Programme of Single-class Village School, 1952

Morning Programme

9   Assembly. Prayers.

9.10   Registration.
         Free Activities (out of doors when possible).
         Washing hands. Preparations for Milk.

9.45   Milk
         Followed by Reading, Writing, Number (for older children).
         For 3-, 4- and 5-year-olds:
             Domestic Activities; Doll and House Play; Building Blocks; Sand and
             Water Play: Shops; Picture Books.

10.45   Recreation.

10.55   Continuing 3 R's work (older children).
             For 3-, 4- and 5-year-olds:
                 Play with material leading to 3 R's, including Home-made Picture
             Books; Drawing Pictures and Patterns; Number Games and Rhymes;
             Apparatus for Counting, Elementary Weighing and Measuring.

11.30   Physical Training.

11.45   Story (including Scripture Story).

Afternoon Programme

1.30   Registration.

1.35   Rest Time for under 5's.
         Quiet Time, Nature Interests, Talks and Discussions for older children.

1.55   Free Activities, including:
             Centres of Interest; Knitting and Sewing connected with Centres of
             Interest; Toy Play; Painting; Modelling; Woodwork; Weighing and
             Measuring; Jigsaw Puzzles; Quiet Corner—Library Books.

2.45   Recreation.

2.55–   Music, Poetry, Story.
3.30

Programme E, included by courtesy of the Director
of Education for Kesteven (Lincolnshire), shows how the
teacher of a small village school adapts her programme
to the needs of her single class of about twenty children
aged three to seven years.

It is interesting to note the basic similarity between
programmes C and E, though the schools represented
are as widely different as possible in size, locality and
organisation.

A consideration of the pursuits or "subjects" within the
framework of the programme directs attention to one of

the most striking differences between the kindergarten and the infant school, a difference almost as marked today as it was a hundred years ago.

The kindergarten has already been referred to as a school not based upon books, whereas the avowed purpose of the early infant schools was (apart from minding children) to give instruction in the elements of the three R's. The bookish tradition of the infant school is so strong that teachers have often felt at a loss to know how to occupy children who were not bent over their books for the greater part of the day. The statement, not infrequently heard, that until a child can read he can do nothing reveals an appallingly cramped idea of what education really is—or of what the child is, for that matter!

In Froebel's writings and in the practice of his followers, the child is seen spending his time and developing his powers by contact with nature, with people and with objects. This is not the place to discuss the "gifts", their symbolism and their function in the development of Froebel's doctrine of innate ideas, but it should be noted that, stripped of their symbolism, they reveal themselves, together with the occupation materials, as the time-less playthings of childhood. Throughout the ages children have played and will continue to play with balls, bricks, sand, clay, the simple constructive materials of paper, card and wood, and the tools that go with them. Not only are those the eternal toys of childhood, they are also the counterparts of those materials and tools used by man in the building up of his social, economic and artistic life. The songs and games of childhood were collected by Froebel, and modelled by him on the traditional games of the homes and villages of his native Thuringia. In this sense there was no artificiality in the material used by Froebel; the artificiality was in the treatment of the material. Probably the most influential thinker to make this criticism of Froebel's work was John Dewey. It is thirty-five years since his essays from "The Elementary School Record" were published in this country in *The School and the Child*, edited by J. J. Findlay, Sarah Fielden Professor of Education in the University of Manchester. In the essay on play and games, Dewey suggests that in the "worship of the external doings discussed by Froebel we have ceased to be loyal to his principle".[1] Those who were privileged to work under Professor Findlay in the Fielden Demonstration School can never forget the adventure of setting aside the time-honoured ritual of gifts, occupations and finger plays and, as Dewey taught, "of getting suggestions from any and from every source". This critical attitude was not only being put to the test in the Fielden School, it was being carried into the elementary (infant and junior) schools, principally in the West Riding of Yorkshire, through sessional courses and a summer school for teachers in which the tutors were often members of the Fielden School staff.

The content of the kindergarten programme was up to this time an alternation between "gifts", "occupations", finger plays, singing games, talks on matters of childish interest in home, school or neighbourhood, stories, and play in the open air. All this was planned, supervised and directed by the teacher and, as has already been said, was for the morning only. The school arts—reading, writing and number—made no appearance in the programme for the group of children of varying ages to about 6 plus years.

In contrast to this, in the infant school no child was considered too young to repeat the letters of the alphabet or their sounds, and to trace their shapes in sand or upon boards. Figures were introduced at an equally early age; in fact, when practical materials, such as sand, clay, etc., were introduced, they were treated chiefly as handmaids of the three R's.

[1] *The School and the Child*, p. 49.

The kindergarten gifts and occupations found their way fairly early into some of the infant schools, but they were introduced as an addition, a trimming, a pleasant relaxation after the serious business of learning to read, write and figure. Until comparatively recent years, it was not uncommon to find the word "kindergarten" entered three or four times a week as a subject of the afternoon time-table! Originally, no doubt, some attempt was made to use the gifts as intended by Froebel—manipulated in a given order to the accompaniment of rhymes and songs, but it is to be doubted whether many of the infant school teachers who used them read much if anything of Froebel's educational theory.

This is very much how matters stood when, in the early years of the present century, some of the infant schools were roused to action by the challenge of the Montessori method.

The claim that children educated by this method "exploded" into reading no doubt played a big part in the appeal but, looking back over the last forty years, it is not in the teaching of reading that the Montessori method has made its greatest mark on our infant schools.

The claim that the didactic apparatus was self-educative had the effect of breaking up classes and of giving children freedom, within strictly defined limits, to follow independently their chosen occupations—this was the beginning of what has been a revolutionary change in infant school method.

But the Montessori apparatus was expensive and the rules of copyright were strict. Infant teachers, however, are nothing if not resourceful, so there descended on the schools an avalanche of home-made apparatus at first roughly following the Montessori pattern, but presently modified and developed according to the needs of the moment and the ingenuity, skill and patience of the teacher. Children in large numbers were set free from a good deal of direct teacher-guidance, and vast amounts of apparatus were needed to take its place.

But this is only half the story. The Montessorians strongly repudiated the notion of play as the child's natural mode of living and learning. The child, they said, was eminently serious; he only played if there were nothing better to do—his world was real, not imaginative. This was a direct challenge to the Froebelians, who were ready to stake their educational reputation upon their belief in the paramount importance of play and imagination in the child's life.

Meanwhile a new and most significant factor was entering unobtrusively upon the educational scene. Psychologists of high standing were making detailed and objective studies of growth and development in the early years of childhood. Arnold Gesell in America and Susan Isaacs in England may be mentioned as pioneers and acknowledged leaders in the new field. Neither they nor their colleagues and followers sought to establish a new method in education, still less to endow it with their own names. Their work was a challenge to teachers to make a critical survey of the methods to which they were accustomed, and to apply the knowledge of child development now placed at their disposal to build up not "*a* method" but methods suited to the children and the circumstances with which they were called upon to deal.

It is hardly too much to say that with this change in outlook a new educational era was entered upon. It marked the emancipation of the teacher as well as of the child and called for a higher level of intellectual ability than had been demanded by the following of a set system, however abstruse its theory. Whether Froebel himself would consider that with the complete abandonment of the gifts, occupations, finger plays and other hall-marks of his doctrine his influence was at an end is difficult to say. Probably he would. But if it is really true that while the letter killeth the spirit giveth life, it may be possible, by taking a longer and a wider view, to see the Froebelian spirit operating in the best of our infant schools today.

If the independent kindergartens can claim to be still true to the spirit of Froebel, so surely can those infant schools which have sought to make use of the psychological knowledge thus placed at their disposal. Between these schools and the kindergartens there is probably less difference as regards the matter and method of their education than at any other time in the century under review.

The numbers in the infant school classes are larger and classification according to age and ability is probably more rigid than in most kindergartens, but the pattern of the education given in each is more marked by similarity than by difference.

After the opening of school a large space of time is usually given in all classes. This may vary in length according to the age of the children and other circumstances, from about an hour or a little less for the youngest children to possibly ninety minutes for the elder ones. In the nursery and admission classes (ages 3 to 5 plus years), the children spend this time in undirected play in classrooms and in the adjacent outdoor play space. Their playthings include the elemental materials—water, sand, clay, with simple tools and utensils to enrich and develop the play; playthings for the exercise of bodily growth and control, climbing and scrambling apparatus, balls, ropes, empty boxes, planks, motor tyres, and a variety of wheeled vehicles. The above playthings are typically used out of doors. Both in and out of doors bricks and blocks take a prominent place. They are large, plain and solid, and lend themselves to the building of houses, railways, boats, garages and the like. A simple screen play-house with its complement of small furniture, dolls, household utensils and prams is usually much in demand by the girls, who may extend their house play to include a general store for shopping excursions or a hospital. To give scope for constructive play of a more permanent nature, there may be a light woodwork bench with tools and scraps of wood, simple interlocking toys, a sewing basket. There will certainly be a dressing-up box. Light easels with large sheets of paper, poster paints and large brushes are much used in the production of those vigorous and lively works of art in which young children excel. There is a corner where picture books are available, and opportunity is provided for children to use pencils and paper and to play some of the simpler counting games. It probably should be noted here that at the time of writing pressure on school accommodation has in some areas led to the exclusion of children under five from the primary schools, but this type of provision is still in many schools available for the entrants' class at the age of five.

During the first time period the children group themselves freely according to the play interest of the moment. After a break for milk and toilet, the remainder of the morning is divided into periods for music, story and verse, possibly some directed physical activity or a more directly controlled form of constructive or manipulative play.

Where dinner is taken in school, the children leave their morning occupations shortly before noon, allowing time for toilet as well as the preparation of the room for dinner. Teachers of young children do not, as a rule, see any difficulty in treating the school day as a complete unit in which preparation for dinner, the serving and taking of the meal, and the period of rest or relaxation which follows it have their educational significance equally with the children's other occupations. The afternoon session follows a pattern similar to the morning, opening with about forty-five to sixty minutes of undirected play, followed by shorter directed periods for music, art or literature. The period set aside for religious instruction is not uncommonly taken at the close of the morning or afternoon session.

With Froebel's ideals in mind, it may be noted that nature experience has not been mentioned in the above description. This problem in town schools has already been referred to in the discussion on buildings. Where some garden has been made available, use is made of this by the children in their play. Visits to parks are fraught with difficulties and even dangers; but it is a rare classroom indeed that is not adorned the year round with flowers and plants brought by teacher and children. Living creatures can be and often are introduced and kept for longer or shorter periods, the care of them being, under supervision, in the hands of the children. Books, pictures and objects of interest, e.g. shells, birds' nests, tree fruits, magnets and prisms are rarely lacking to add to the wealth of experience of the young inquirers.

Here is a framework within which "living with our children" is indeed a reality. It would be difficult to think of a phrase more apt to describe the unfailing freshness of the vitality which carries children and teachers along together through ever-widening fields of growth and discovery.

This account of the work with the youngest children has been given in some detail because although the content varies, the framework remains fairly constant, not only through the infant stage of education but, most happily, in some schools through the junior stage as well.

Naturally, as the children grow older the time periods become rather longer in duration, and with lengthened span of interest and attention come development and growth of interest to include mastery of the basic skills and knowledge of man's achievements in space and in time.

The first time period therefore may be occupied in the pursuit of an interest—shared by the whole class in, for example, a matter of local history, local industry, local government; the provision of clothing, food or shelter throughout the ages, or possibly the production of a play, puppet show or book. Any of these pursuits, it may be seen, will involve the children in inquiries by visits, letters or reading—in the recording of their discoveries or in re-discovering for themselves processes such as spinning, weaving, building. Skills are thus required, children need to read, to write, to measure or compute, and in another block of time following perhaps a shorter interval for class singing or physical exercise, the children will devote themselves to the mastery of these skills, divided into groups dictated by mutual interest or ability.

As the power of social adjustment and co-operation grows, the children are increasingly able to sink individual preferences in favour of group experiences, whether it be in the field of music, games or literature.

A reference has been made to the junior stage of education. No greater mistake could be made than to think of Froebel as an educator of little children only. His work with older children pre-dated by many years his invention of the "kindergarten". But the English conception of education—apart from the work of the great public schools—has always stressed instruction in what have become known, almost officially, as the three R's. To this conception the scholarship system has added weight so that any type of education that was not obviously and avowedly directed to the attainment of scholarships (rather than scholarship) was regarded with the greatest suspicion. Even the infant schools have had to make a firm stand against this point of view, and perhaps the courage shown by many teachers in these schools in resisting the scholarship pressure has not been sufficiently appreciated.

However, a more enlightened view of the junior stage has not been altogether lacking. A landmark was reached in 1931 by the publication of the Hadow Report entitled *The Junior School*. Here was a charter indeed for children of the 7–11 age-group.

There were many reasons, no doubt, why it fell so largely on deaf ears. "The curriculum should be thought of in terms of activity . . ." may have become a commonplace of speech, but it remained largely to "be thought of", hardly, if ever, to be acted upon.

There were, however, teachers who set rare but shining examples of what a junior school may be when animated by this spirit of activity—it would be invidious to mention names, but reference must be made to one piece of work which has had perhaps the greatest single influence in vitalising the work of the junior schools. This is the work achieved through the teachers' part-time courses organised by the University of Durham Department of Education—now the Institute of Education—in preparing teachers for the Certificate of the National Froebel Foundation. Qualified teachers in both infant and junior schools from a wide area around Newcastle and Durham have attended these courses, sacrificing the whole of their Saturdays for classes in education and art and for conferences and discussions among themselves. This has been a truly evangelical piece of work; not infrequently a teacher attending the courses has been the means of interesting his or her colleagues until there is now a considerable body of teachers in that area strongly united by common experience and unity of purpose who are demonstrating, not only through the work in their classrooms but by their own vitality and enthusiasm, what a curriculum thought of (and acted upon) in terms of activity and experience may achieve.

It must not be thought that this is by any means an isolated example, or even the first in time, of such work.

It is used here as an example because the writer's contact from time to time over a period of years with the work in Newcastle has given a first-hand experience from which it is possible to write with warmth and confidence.

The teacher is of course the determining factor in any piece of educational work, and it is now time to consider the teacher herself and her function in the early kindergartens and in contemporary infant schools, and to see what changes time has brought about in both institutions.

There will be no surprise in the discovery that the teacher a hundred years ago was the leader, director and controller of all the children's activities whether in kindergarten or infant school. It is true that Froebel sternly denounced what he called "prescriptive, categorical, interfering" education, and decreed that instruction and training should be "passive, following (only guarding and protecting)". But then he invented a system of complicated exercises with balls, bricks, paper and other materials, not to mention finger plays and singing games, which necessitated direction and leadership by a teacher. A glimpse of the games is given in an account by Froebel's great-niece, Henrietta Breymann (later Frau Schrader), of the Rudolstadt Convention in the closing years of Froebel's life. After the morning session, at which Froebel had discoursed on the symbolism of the games, the afternoon was given over to practical demonstrations. Fräulein Breymann describes how the children, marching and singing, were led in by the kindergartners to demonstrate the ring games. Apparently there was some criticism and even ridicule on the part of the onlookers, and even Fräulein Breymann, devoted admirer though she was, confesses her inability to understand how playing *according to directions* [1] could make men

---

[1] Italics mine.

noble. To her the idea seemed "narrow, limited and un-natural".

That the children's games were directed in a spirit of gentleness and persuasion and without prescriptive categorical interference is undoubted, but direction there certainly must have been. The games and occupations, however, were far closer to the natural instincts and interests of childhood than were the letters and figures upon which the little ones in the contemporary infant school were obliged to spend their time in uncomfortable cramped positions. Not only the children but the teacher felt the strain of this unnatural concentration, and on her devolved the responsibility of producing prescribed results for the head teacher's or inspector's examination. If her tone was sometimes sharpened or her words underlined by an occasional tap with the ruler, she surely deserves sympathy before censure.

While in kindergartens and infant schools alike the need for the specialised training of teachers has always been recognised, there has been an ever-present tendency to regard a relatively low standard of attainment as sufficient for the needs of an infant school. The elementary nature of the instruction given, coupled with the immaturity of the pupils, has encouraged the idea that intellectual attainment was wasted in an infant teacher. In 1904, as a result of a report of five women inspectors appointed by the (then) Board of Education to inquire into the admission of infants to public elementary schools and on the curriculum suitable for children under five, the Chief Inspector decided that while recognising the desirability of special training for infant teachers, nevertheless, "two supplementary teachers of good motherly instincts might be as good for sixty babies under five as one clever certificated teacher".

The training of infant teachers in the two-year training colleges has presented some features of interest and

In the Playground, 1952

significance in the development of the pattern of education in infant schools. Many years before the recognition
of the Certificate of the National Froebel Union (later
Foundation) by the (then) Board of Education for grant
purposes, women holding this certificate were employed
as lecturers in infant method in the two-year colleges.
The students coming under their influence not only
received a training with a strongly Froebelian bias, but
also became imbued with a very fine sense of vocation.
They were usually a minority group in the college, with
their work more specialised than that of the larger com-
posite junior-senior group. They were, as a rule, the less
intellectually able members of the student body, but
their devotion to their work and a reputation for practical ability and common sense gave them an acknowledged standing with their fellow-students and with the
staff. The growth of the new psychology of young
children, however, coupled with the rapid development
of the nursery school movement, had a marked influence
on the quality of the students who chose to be trained as
infant teachers. In the early 1920s it became by no means
unusual for the ablest students of a college "year" to be
found in the infants section. These very able and even
distinguished students, passing into the infant schools
and becoming, in due time, headmistresses, training
college lecturers and inspectors, have to a great extent
been the means of making the infant school what it is
today. The growth has been from within, and has been
not unworthy of Froebel himself and of the great leaders
who first spread his doctrines in this country.

The twenty years immediately preceding the outbreak
of the 1939 War were golden years for the infant school,
but children are the first victims of war, and today it will
take great courage, determination and skill even to hold
what has been gained in the face of the restrictions which
threaten education on every front. That the struggle will

be gallant is assured, for the heart as well as the brains of the infant teacher is in her work.

By tradition the teacher has been one who works apart. The high railings and padlocked gates of the old School Board buildings were not there by accident, nor were they merely parts of an architectural design; they had a dual function—to keep the children in and the rest of the world out. It is right and proper that the schoolmaster should be monarch in his own domain, but not by force. The last twenty-five years have seen an unlocking of the gates and a lowering of the barriers, making an easy passage between school and community in both directions. The need for contact with nature and living creatures and for space in which to play has stimulated teachers of little children to take their children out of doors whenever possible. Not only have walks been taken to near-by parks, but visits have been paid to local craftsmen, the blacksmith, the baker or to a not-too-distant farm. The disappearance of crafts in an increasingly mechanised civilisation is not only robbing childhood of one of its joys, but is casting a veil of obscurity over the basic realities upon which life is built. How to redress this balance is one of the problems which faces the teacher today.

Older children can and do pay profitable visits to the more complicated factories and workshops of today, and in turn receive as visitors in the school workers who come to tell them about their daily work. Milkmen, postmen and others find themselves under a fire of questions when they have described their daily duties, while Members of Parliament and civic dignitaries have found it well worth while to discuss with older children their responsibilities and duties.

Contact between home and school is easiest and most natural where little children are concerned. Froebel addressed a large part of his educational writing to parents; we know that they were welcomed in the school at Keilhau. Mothers naturally bring their little ones to school, at any rate for the first time, and are generally glad of an opportunity to establish a friendly contact with the teacher, who usually comes to mean so much in the children's lives. School meals and medical inspection have strengthened this bond, for unless there is mutual confidence and understanding between parents and teachers these services, transferred from home to school, will disrupt instead of strengthening a child's life. In many cases these informal meetings have grown into parent-teacher associations. One such gathering reached a high-water mark of mutual friendliness when parents, grandparents, teachers, managers and the school caretaker met to discuss with a visiting speaker the value of play in the child's school life. Needless to say, this was in an infant school.

The more important aspects of school life have been passed in review as an attempt has been made to trace the effects of Froebelian doctrine in the primary schools of our day. But to leave them thus separated would be to miss the whole point. "In all things there lives and reigns an eternal law," says Froebel in the opening words of *The Education of Man*. This law is based on an eternal Unity—this Unity is God. Froebel saw the "vision of redeemed humanity, living in harmony with nature, governed by love and rejoicing in ever-progressing creative work".[1] He believed, moreover, in the progressive growth and development of humanity. It would be contrary to the essence of his teaching if Froebelian practice in our schools today were to be found exactly as he left it. This has not been so, but his doctrine, like the leaven in a measure of meal, has worked quietly and unobtrusively. We cannot claim that the whole is leavened, but as we review the work of our primary schools today we

[1] Introduction to *Sketches of Froebel's Life and Times*.

can recognise the growth of a tendency towards unification, a bringing together—teachers and pupils come together as fellow-workers and adventurers, sharing the delights of discovery in nature, in the works of man and in their own growing powers. The "subjects" of the school fuse together as they are seen to be but different facets of man's life in the world and his growth towards heaven. Barriers which in the past have isolated the school from the life of the world around it are breaking down—children go out to discover not only the works of nature but also the works of man, while workers and parents are welcome visitors and co-operators within the school—and the child himself is, in modern educational parlance, a "whole" child. The whole of him is welcomed in school—the active, inquiring, curious, talkative and restless parts of him no less than the more studious and docile parts. The successful school is the school which embraces all these elements, welding them into a lively, vigorous community such as was no doubt in Froebel's mind when he uttered his famous appeal: "Kommt lasst uns unsern Kindern leben!" [1]

[1] *The Education of Man,* International Education Series, p. 89.

CHAPTER IV

THE INFLUENCE OF FROEBEL ON THE INDEPENDENT PREPARATORY SCHOOLS OF TODAY

I

INTERCHANGE and development of ideas should nowhere be more felt than in schools, and a hundred years after his death the question arises: how far are we doing this or that because we follow Froebel? Is not a particular practice due rather to Montessori, Dewey, or even to Plato or Comenius? Certainly one of the good things a Froebel training does for its students is to open their minds to the ideas of other great educators as well, and that is why many teachers call their schools Progressive rather than Froebelian. The problem at this date is to point to a school or a practice and say with certainty: "That at least is Froebelian." In this chapter, therefore, it seems best to take certain ideas set out by Froebel (chiefly in *The Education of Man*) and try to see how they are being interpreted today in schools which are run by teachers brought up in his theory of education.

At this point someone might ask: "How many Froebel schools are there in Britain today?" This is a question hard to answer. There are eleven which have been inspected and registered as Froebel Schools by the National Froebel Foundation, but there are also many besides these. There is nothing (unfortunately) to prevent any school from calling itself a Froebel school, and at times when Froebel education is fashionable, many so-called Froebel schools exist whose methods would not be at all in line with those advocated by the National Froebel Foundation. Conversely, many schools which make no mention of Froebel in their titles are consciously trying to educate children as he would have wished: others are staffed by teachers trained in one or other of the Froebel training colleges who almost unconsciously see their educational problems from a Froebelian angle: yet again there is many a school—county primary as well as independent—whose methods and atmosphere are truly Froebelian, though they would call themselves Progressive. As is made clear in Chapter II, the leaven of Froebel's ideas has spread wide because students trained in Froebel colleges have gone out to train others in colleges not specially training in his name; so his way of thought has largely coloured all training of infant teachers lately except that which is specifically Montessori or P.N.E.U. Where teachers are not cramped by a false tradition but are allowed to develop their technique in such a way that the school is a harmony in which children may grow by creative activity, there you are likely to get a true Froebel school. By its fruits you must judge it.

Froebel gives as his aim that he wants to "train up free thinking independent men". For him, man only achieves full stature when, as a child of God, he can live harmoniously in relation to the spiritual and the natural world.

The name he gave his school for the young—"kindergarten"—is in itself a parable for parent and teacher, and bears out his saying that it is development and not moulding or forcing which is the real agent in education.

In *The Education of Man*, section 8, he says: "We grant time and space to young plants and animals because we know that, in accordance with the laws that live in them, they will develop properly and grow well; young animals and plants are given rest, and arbitrary interference with their growth is avoided, because it is known that the opposite practice would disturb their pure unfolding and sound development; but the young human being is looked upon as a piece of wax, a lump of clay, which man can mould into what he pleases."

The simile of the child and the vine, in some form or other, is probably the piece of Froebel's teaching most deeply felt—even if rarely expressed—by teachers who own his influence, for they must regard themselves as gardeners watching development, ready to feed the growth, ready to prune, restrain or weed according to need; trying to help each child to grow to the best he may be; not worried to make all the plants the same, but trying to bring it about that they shall grow, so that the whole garden shall be a harmony.

Froebel laid down certain essentials for the healthy growth and development of children, and these may be resolved into five main headings.

1. Self-activity.
2. Connectedness and unbroken continuity.
3. Creativeness.
4. Physical activity.
5. Happy and harmonious surroundings.

The Education of Man is itself full of delightful examples of what Froebel meant by these terms, and since the natural activities of young children change remarkably little with the passing of a century, it is indeed difficult to give any examples more modern than those of the author himself; but let us here look at some illustrations taken from British schools today.

1. *Self-activity*

"At an early period the child should learn, apply and practise the most difficult of all arts—to hold fast the centre and fulcrum of his life in spite of all digressions, disturbances and hindrances" (*The Education of Man*, section 19).

"He won't concentrate." "What you need to teach her is concentration—she is intelligent enough." This is the all too frequent cry of parents today, and they are speaking of children who have not found, or cannot use, that steady centre of their inner life, that core of interest within themselves, on which to build their pattern of life.

In activity that springs from an inner urge, a kitten learns to run and jump. We say that it is playing, but we know also that without this play it could never grow into an efficient cat. In any good nursery class you may see this self-activity in which the young children are developing their powers.

Three children are playing at the water-tank. For twenty minutes a three-year-old boy pours water from a kettle through a cullender. He does not talk, he just watches the water falling from the spout to the cullender and from the holes in the cullender back into the tank. He refills the kettle, pours and watches again. He is wrapt in his own meditations and feelings and has no interest to spare for the two four-year-old boys beside him who are pouring water through a funnel into a long tube and suddenly realise that the water comes out of the tube differently according as they raise or lower the funnel. The embryo physicists call excitedly to their teacher to see how the water spurts up and dies down. It is likely that one day soon they will find out how a siphon works, but though that may be useful when later they study science, it is not in the laws of siphonage that the value of this water play lies.

In the quiet corner with the little round table and low chairs behind the screen, Bennie, aged 4½, has taken a picture book from the shelves and is "reading" to Julia, aged 4. True, the words he says are not exactly those printed opposite the picture, but they hold Julia, and there is no need for any teacher to tell her to "attend" or Bennie to "get on". For both of them at this moment are "reading", and that means to them getting pleasure from a book.

Outside the open door Jacob (who is new and yesterday wept when his mother left) is watching children walk along the little wall surrounding the sand-pit. It is only raised ten inches, but the top is rounded and to the children it is at first an adventure in balancing. He is torn between fear and desire. A more confident child half-way along the wall wobbles and quickly grasps the teacher's hand involuntarily stretched out to steady her. When the teacher turns round, Jacob stands perched unsteadily on the corner of the wall. "Help *me*," he demands. His hand in hers, tense with anxiety, he reaches the end of the little wall and jumps down. He wastes no words, indeed he has none adequate, but the great sigh of relief, the firm mouth and shining eyes tell of the size of the achievement in his life. "Help me, please," he says, and this time there is confidence, not terror, in the request. Soon it will be, "I can do it alone," and Jacob will begin to feel that the nursery is his. A short way away Ian is hanging upside down by his knees from the climbing frame shouting to everyone, "Look at me." Nancy on the swing is asking a larger child to push "Harder! Harder!" But Jacob who before would have gazed at both in unhappy envy or wonder, now gives them no more than the cursory glance that courtesy or interest demand. He, too, has his value. He can walk along the wall. Soon he will run like that big boy. He must practise. Up again! Life is a serious business.

Stephen has come wandering out to find his teacher; he is nearly five and much interested in words and names. He draws her back to where he is working. "Look!" he says with conscious pride as he posts them through the shaped holes in a box. "There goes the square. There goes the triangle. There goes the cylinder."

A small group of children are playing "mothers and

fathers" in the house corner. They keep up a flow of conversation in imitation of their own parents—ordering, organising, explaining, learning to get on with each other, and learning much more. In their own world they are oblivious of all else around them. If they want sand for their buns, they go and fetch it without a look at Jacob and his grand achievement.

Twenty-five children all "self-active"—doing what they themselves feel is the important thing, playing, imitating, practising, but, while the interest lasts, completely wrapt up in what they are doing, unmoved by noise or motion around them, absorbed, concentrating.

Not all children in the nursery have this natural concentration, in some it has already been maimed. Children whose life from the earliest day has been lived to the pattern imposed from without; children who have been impatiently snatched from a self-chosen occupation to fit in with some plan beyond their understanding; children who have been denied any freedom to act for themselves or who have been stifled by overmuch outward stimulation—these have had no chance to learn to pursue their own ends patiently and quietly. They wander aimlessly, they make wrong use of materials, they attract attention to themselves, until they feel secure enough in the new environment to make a tentative effort to do something by themselves for themselves. Then slowly from a very small beginning they are transformed into serious workers pursuing—of their own volition—some course which they know within themselves to be worth while for them.

It is easy to see in the nursery class how self-activity is a natural force in education. Even the most anxious parent can recognise that in his play and self-directed practising a three-year-old is learning.

"Up to the age of six," said Froebel, "a child is learning to differentiate between himself and the rest of the world. He is learning about the possibilities in himself and his surroundings, he is learning to designate correctly the objects and actions of his daily life. He is experiencing those attributes of the spirit which will later lead him to an understanding of his need for God."

All this is easy to see, but it appears to be much more difficult for adults to realise that our nature is so made that it continues to develop of its own volition right on through infancy and youth. Those teachers, however, who adapt their ideals and methods to make use of the child's natural urge to grow up, find that what they have begun in faith (and often a feeble, doubting faith) carries them forward in the flood of the children's enthusiasm far faster than they expected. True, it needs some courage because the self-directed activity of children does not follow necessarily the lines laid down by traditional education; but there is no doubt that the study of psychology is very gradually educating those who rule our examination systems, and the demands made upon children's mental attainment are slowly beginning to correspond to the rate of an average child's development.

One of the great advantages of the independent over the council school is that a child may stay in one school over a longer period, even in some cases from the age of 3 to 13 years, and this gives a much better chance of seeing how certain educational ideas work out, than when a child must be prepared for a change of school at, say, 5 and 11 years. It is becoming increasingly apparent that children who develop along lines of their own guided but self-generated activity, continue their studies with gathering momentum; whereas the child who has been crammed and forced during his junior school-days frequently flags and loses interest in his work by the age of 16 or 17. Grammar school teachers know all too well how often the bright well-crammed little scholar of the entry form, having managed to matriculate, sinks into weary apathy in the sixth form, while the lead is taken by children who had been too stolid and independent to be flogged into early brilliance.

It is easy, then, to see how self-activity is an important factor in the education of children under 6, and we have proof of the evils of the lack of it, in the sixth forms of our grammar schools and in the lack of direction and enthusiasm of the lives of all too many adults.

Let us now try to see how the self-activity of a child works in the junior school, and perhaps even more importantly in that class known as the transition which caters for what is, indeed, a period of change—the seven-year-old stage, when babyhood is being left behind and the boy or girl begins to emerge. We call it "the seven-year-old stage", and it is marked by a delightful toothlessness, but it is a stage of development which often stretches over the period from 6 to 8, or even 9, years.

The self-activity of children in the transition stage is very diverse. Perhaps its chief characteristic is physical activity. The energy of the seven-year-old is proverbial. Small wonder that he becomes fidgety if condemned to spend most of his day sitting on a school bench. Left to himself, he climbs trees or their playground equivalents, he gangs up with his fellows, builds camps and organises attacks on other gangs. He pries into hedges and ditches. At one moment he is the most efficient domestic worker in the home, at another he is making a distressing mess with his collections of oddments and his complete disregard of mud on his boots. He accepts and feels secure in an ordered routine, yet he is always anxious to escape at bed-time, and frequently is late for meals because he was absorbed in some important employment of his own. In between his bursts of physical activity come periods of passivity, resting times, thinking times. Few audiences are more satisfying to the story-teller than these transition children, with their enthusiasms, ready laughter or deep solemnity. These are the children who will tell you when the first snowdrop is out or where the nests are hidden; these are the children who coming in from a boisterous game will suddenly surprise one by a penetrating question about the nature of God or what Heaven is like. In school, the environment and the guidance of the teacher seek to use the energy of these children so that they may develop those sides of their nature which will help them "to be free-thinking independent men and women".

The children come to school in the morning full of ideas of what they are to do. Most of them have been awake since dawn planning their day. The question now is: are they to set aside their plans for a while and attend to the sort of work adults think necessary while they are fresh and untired; or shall they first attend to their own plans and later practise the skills necessary for a growing child?

Froebel himself thought it better to let the period of self-activity precede the period of directed activity, and most schools today which have tried it find it works better this way round.

Self-activity at this stage is very different from the self-activity of the nursery class. It is more purposive, the children are far more apt to be working as groups to produce something; and those children who are practising have usually set themselves a task in one of the skills of reading, writing or arithmetic, leaving the practice of physical skill for a playtime or an out-of-door period. The interplay between lessons and the self-activity periods are now obvious. Sometimes the spontaneous interest of the children gives rise to a course of lessons, and sometimes a lesson spurs the children to a piece of self-chosen work beyond what the teacher would ordinarily demand. This happened when a Greek story so caught the imagination of a seven-year-old girl that she appeared at school next morning with the Greek alphabet which she had made her father copy out for her. Copying out the Greek alphabet became the rage that morning, and in the evening fathers—surprised by the interest of their offspring in things classical—brought forth scraps of knowledge from their own school-days, and felt a pleasant possibility of a strange new unity of interest with their children. Pictures, scraps of information, accounts of Mediterranean cruises flowed into the classroom. One group of children began to build a model of a Greek temple, others wanted to read and write and illustrate more Greek stories; yet others were caught by the interest of a new alphabet and began to think about letters and how different peoples wrote, and so came on their first conscious thought about language.

In another class a child's imagination was caught when her teacher told of the early Britons making coracles of willow and hide. The next morning the eight-year-old girl arrived at school with a great bunch of withes from the willow tree in her garden, and for several days she and a boy laboured to make a coracle with willow and with paper for hides. It was a difficult task and the teacher's help was needed, but when it was finished the child had that feeling of achievement which is the reward of a purpose carried out. She had added to her faith in her own powers, and had acquired a deeper understanding of the problems of her early forefathers.

In the period given to self-activity some children will be drawing, painting, sewing or modelling, some will be working because they really have an urge to express an idea; one may be making a birthday present, another completing a piece of work begun in another lesson. A child who has just mastered a new process in arithmetic or who has made a step forward in reading or writing will often be found at this time practising the newly acquired skill.

One summer term for several weeks a whole class used most of the activity periods in constructing and furnishing a caravan. It was made of orange boxes and some old pram wheels, and painted with gay patterns. It was furnished with a carpet, a kettle, bench and table and other necessities. The caravan was a great bond between the children; they did not actually play in it much, but they talked of it and planned for it incessantly, and were very proud of showing it to people, which was not surprising since it always aroused wonder and praise.

This piece of work had grown from the interest of one or two children, who were captivated by a story of life in a caravan. It cannot be pretended that the majority of the class all had the idea of making a caravan. It was not in that sense originally *self*-activity on the part of each one. One child said, "Couldn't we make a caravan?" Others said "let's", and the teacher no doubt fostered the idea; but the measure in which it was adopted by the rest of the class could be seen from the way in which they talked of it, worked for it and brought materials for it from home.

The question that anxious parents ask is, whether the school is justified in allowing the children to play like this in lesson time when important examinations loom ahead for them at the age of 11, 12 or 13 years. Should not the children play at home and work in school, they ask. They do not consider sufficiently that the child who can play well can also work well; that the habits of work are formed in play, for then a child is directing himself; he sets himself a task and carries it through. There is, or should be, opportunity for richer and more stimulating play in school than at home. A child at home may grow dull in his play, and continue going over the same thing instead of progressing to more complicated or purposeful play, as he is likely to do in a fellowship of children, where there is interchange of ideas. The child who has ambitious parents may, on the other hand, set himself a standard (even in his play) which is too high for him. He cannot carry through his purpose successfully because he lacks the skill, but is afraid to try simpler things for fear of disappointing his parents. He becomes often a grand talker, outlining wonderful projects, but they come to nothing; and he arrives at school with a butterfly mind, as little prepared for work as for play. Even the child who, unspoilt and natural, has the ability to play well, often lacks long enough periods at a stretch under modern conditions at home, and, moreover, a Froebel school which cares about play can, as a rule, provide a more stimulating environment for productive play—companions, materials, space, tools.

But the child in the transition class is very much concerned with growing up. He often feels small, powerless and inefficient. He is eager to learn to read and write and study, but, being often intensely proud, he is afraid to seem too eager, lest it shall prove too difficult and he shall seem to fail. Once a child realises that he is getting on, that in lessons as in his play he only has to put his mind to it to make progress, he finds lessons very nearly as delightful as play; indeed, sometimes it is difficult to tell which is play and which is work, since he wants to do both. Here again the child who "plays" in school helps his teacher to show him the point of the work he does in the "lessons".

The child who has been playing at shopping wants to know how to make out bills properly, wants to know how to write advertisements. The nurses in the dolls' hospital need to be able to write down their patients' ailments and keep a temperature chart. The children who were wrapt up in their Greek study were eager to write books about their work. The wise teacher makes use of the play interests to give the children a purpose in the gaining of skills. Thus she supplies a second, short-term incentive

Weighing and Measuring, 1952

Physical Education, 1952

because from a child's point of view it takes a very long time to learn to write or read or do arithmetic.

What happens, then, to the self-activity of a child when he leaves the transition and enters the school proper? Here, according to Froebel, the emphasis changes. The boy begins to realise his own spiritual nature and his own mind, he becomes conscious of the outer visible world, the world of nature and, uniting yet differentiating both, he becomes conscious of language. Through mind, nature and language, "the school and instruction are to lead the boy to the threefold, yet in itself one, knowledge —to the knowledge of himself in all his relations, and thus to the knowledge of man as such; to the knowledge of God, the eternal condition, cause and source of his being, and of the being of all things; and to the knowledge of nature and the outer world as proceeding from the Eternal Spirit and depending thereupon." [1]

Here, then, we are to show children the infinite variety of the world in which they live and also the unity that runs through all. Now they are ready to be led forth, their curiosity ranges ever wider, their ambition is more clear. They want teachers who can help them to find the answers to all they want to know. They are becoming increasingly self-critical; they long for instruction to make them more apt. What part does self-activity play now in the school-life of a boy or girl?

Self-activity if it has been used as a principle through the school has, by the time a child is nine or ten, created a habit of mind which now stands him in good stead. He is used to thinking out his own problems and finding means to solve them. He is used to moving freely about the school or garden without disturbing others. He is used to the idea that he can find answers to his questions in books, and that his teacher can direct his search for knowledge. He knows the pleasure that comes from work-

[1] *The Education of Man*, section 59.

ing as one of a group. Above all, that inner urge to do something, which Froebel has called self-activity, is more and more called into being by suggestions for work made by the teacher.

All those of us who teach know the joy of coming on work which is more than a recapitulation of a lesson given. We say (and truly) "he has put himself into this". This same self-activity, which is akin to the feeling of creating, may be shown as well in mathematics or French or Latin as in English or in handwork or art. It means that the pupil has made that part, at least, of the subject his own. It is his for life. It is part of his true education. The inspector of Froebel's school at Keilhau writes of the pupils there in his report: "Everything they take up they must be able to think; and therefore what they cannot think they do not take up." Parents and teachers who really understand this idea do not seek to hurry their children into parrot learning of a subject for which they are not mentally ready.

As children grow towards adolescence they naturally are more separated from their teachers, and much of their own creative work may be kept private to themselves. It is most often seen in the poems they write, the pictures they paint, and often in voluntary work they do in connection with a school subject that interests them. Two girls handed in nature work done by themselves out of school hours. One was an account of her dog, his breed and nature, rules for his health, his feeding—indeed, a fairly complete manual on boxer bull-terriers, illustrated with her own drawings, tracings, snapshots and pictures cut from papers. The other child had kept a diary, illustrated, of the growth of plants and trees in the school drive throughout the spring term.

The following poem was the result of an actual experience which a twelve-year-old girl happened to share with her form mistress. On an evening of golden light they

were both in the school orchard when the trees were in
blossom. Each realised that the bird's song against such
a background was to her a moment of supreme experience. The teacher later found this poem in the child's
own book of verses:

> *I walk along the garden path,*
> *Guess what I espy.*
> *A Blackbird strutting on the lawn*
> *Quite nearby.*
>
> *I walk a little farther on,*
> *To a place apart,*
> *A chaffinch sitting on a tree,*
> *Sings all his heart.*

The keeping of pets is a very usual form of self-activity
with children aged 10 to 12, and this derives straight from
Froebel himself, along with the practice of gardening. It
is very noticeable that these two occupations are really
inaugurated and kept up by the children themselves
without urging from adults, and it is amazing to see how
much sense of responsibility a well-educated child has
towards her pets, and how unbidden, though with disappointment, she will put the necessity of cleaning out
the rabbit-hutch before any form of amusement. This
sort of self-discipline, unselfishness—call it what you will
—is a quality we want to encourage in our children, and
it is worth remembering that it is a slow growth if it is to
spring from what Froebel calls the inner consciousness of
the child. Parents who think that by giving a rabbit to a
seven-year-old child and telling him to look after it, they
will foster in him a sense of responsibility, are doomed
to disappointment; and if they are not careful—to a dead
rabbit too. Young children love to look after pets for a
time, with help and stimulation from an adult; and this

early training does, in fact, show later in the self-activity of the ten-year-old.

The power to take up into himself ideas from the world around him—from home or school or from nature—and use them later as material for himself to work upon creatively, should be an increasing feature of the development of every child. It is the habit of mind which most of all will lead to a full and happy life. The Froebel school will seek to foster this self-activity by every means in its power, and especially by allowing space on the school timetable for real play and activity which arises from the children's own need and not only from what the teacher thinks they ought to desire. But on the other side the teacher will seek always to give to children the materials and the instruction which may form a basis for their self-activity sooner or later.

For example a group of girls aged 10 to 13 years, who were at boarding-school, decided to rouse a teacher on her birthday morning with a song, which they had written especially for the occasion. It was harmonised and rendered by voices and recorders, and although in the excitement of the moment it was not all perfectly in tune, it gave very great pleasure to all concerned, and was quite an achievement, since no adult had known anything about it beforehand. This group of girls was an able and a musical group, but their feelings could not possibly have taken this form of expression unless they had been taught carefully something of the art of composition of verse and of music, and unless in addition to their singing lessons they had learnt to play the recorder.

The happier the relationship between teacher and taught, the more likely is the teacher to see the results of the self-activity of the child in his own private work, as well as in that prompted by school lessons. In a school where the art is taken entirely by the form teachers, it is noticeable that the art is good or weak—not according to the ability of the teacher in drawing or painting, but according to the social relationship between teacher and children. In fact, the children's paintings act as a sort of barometer of their feelings as a class.

It seems as though the role of self-activity in a school changes as the years go by. For the little child it is the starting-point which drives him forward into study, and then when he approaches adolescence it becomes the expression of the wealth or poverty of the education he is receiving.

Before leaving the subject of this first and most easily recognised of Froebel's principles, a word of caution is necessary. Froebel said:

"The child, the boy, man indeed, should know no other endeavour but to be at every stage of development wholly what this stage calls for. Then will each successive stage spring like a new shoot from a healthy bud; and at each successive stage he will with the same endeavour again accomplish the requirements of this stage: for only the adequate development of man at each preceding stage can effect and bring about adequate development at each succeeding later stage." [1]

The temptation to hurry a child through his stages of growth is very strong in adults. Animal trainers have learnt to go very slowly and patiently in training young animals, but with the infinitely more complex young human being we have not yet acquired the tradition of patient and carefully observant waiting for the right moment to teach a new skill or introduce a new idea. There comes a moment when the carefully nurtured child put into the right environment will reach out for the next stage of his experience, and many a mother and teacher have watched with joyous amazement what happens when with this readiness he takes his next step forward, triumphant and confident. It is all too easy by

[1] *The Education of Man*, section 22.

suggestion or by dissatisfaction to make a young child discontented with his present stage of development so that self-activity dies within him and he strives to do what is expected of him. Clever teaching meeting a good intellect can often teach a child something for which his inner self is not yet ready. The result seems at first wonderful, but some natural growth has been cut off, something in the child is frustrated, some branch will never bear fruit. This is the sort of education which leads to nervousness and what parents delight to call a "highly strung" condition. It is more like a mental form of rickets which will become a trouble when it is too late to make up for a form of starvation in infancy. This is conditioning the type of scholar who in Froebel's words has "a notion that it is possible for him to do wholly without the instruction and training of the preceding stage of development". How often we meet the sort of child who seems incapable of understanding that knowledge of a subject comes by understanding the rudiments and not by some sort of magic. It is for this reason that the Froebel teacher is often hard pressed to stop an over-ambitious parent from hurrying a child too fast through his natural stages of growth. The wise teacher will, however, also be on the alert to see that her pupils have the best and richest opportunities for advancing in experience and satisfying the demands of their inner nature, for she knows that to be held back in growth because of lack of opportunity is also a grave evil.

II

"The school endeavours to render the scholar fully conscious of the nature and inner life of things and of himself, to teach him to know the inner relations of things to one another, to the human being, to the scholar and to the living source and conscious unity of all things —to God." [1]

---

[1] *The Education of Man*, section 56.

It is possible for a pupil to emerge from school thinking that all the subjects he has been taught are as separate in life as they were in the neat sections of the time-table on the classroom wall. It is possible for a parent to say, "But my child has her religion at home, need you teach it in school? I send my child to learn lessons." We all recognise the hopeless case of the adult who has no sense of unity in his life; but even yet we make far too little effort to unify the work in our schools. If religion means anything to us, it is the power which unifies and gives direction to all our activities—which gives a pattern to our life.

In most schools you will find a daily assembly—usually a form of religious service—which is a conscious effort (at least in its origin) to feel this unity. The school assembly seeks not only to give a feeling of unity through the bodily presence of all its members meeting for one purpose—though that in itself is something; it seeks also to give unity to the work and play of the school. If the service is one of praise to the Creator, it is a fit beginning or end to a day spent largely in study of the works of the Creator as seen in nature or in the works and ways of His creature Man.

If the service is one of consecration and dedication, then, again, how can his children serve God better than by learning about Him in his work and by training and developing the powers He has given them?

It is customary to use the school assembly times for announcements, general congratulations and, when necessary, harangues. Often the reason given for this is that it is convenient, for assembly is the one time at which the whole school meets; but surely there is in reality a more fundamental reason, although admittedly it is often forgotten. It is a good thing for children to realise that the whole of their school life has a necessary connection (whether they see it or not) with their religious life. If an announcement, a talk on some behaviour that has fallen short of courtesy, a rejoicing in a match won or a scholarship gained, some arrangement affecting the well-being of the whole school, is not suitable to come directly after the religious service, it is not likely to be fit to be communicated to the whole school at any other time.

The fact that announcements have to be made just after readings, prayers or hymns should ensure that they are treated in a spirit which sees in them a part of the whole training of life.

Apart from the assembly, however, the feeling of what Froebel often calls "connectedness" should underlie all the teaching in the school. The idea of unity is implicit rather than explicit, but it should permeate the atmosphere of the school.

Parents are welcome in a Froebel school because parents and teachers together have at heart the care of the child. Their ideas as to how to bring about his well-being may differ, but since both desire that he shall grow to be the best that he can be, there is every hope that by meeting and discussing difficulties and possibilities, they may come to understand each other and work together for his good. For this purpose schools hold parents' meetings, with lectures on children and education, to be followed by discussion. But in addition to these the parents should know personally and have easy access to all those who teach their children. There is a great difference between the children who feel that their parents and the school are in sympathy and understanding with each other and those who are told one thing at school and the opposite at home. Children quickly adapt themselves to the double life demanded of them by this state of affairs, and so begins in them that double standard which must be responsible for much of the evil of our civilisation.

Some parents find it easy to co-operate with the school. They give generously of their understanding, time and encouragement; others—probably many of these were unhappy themselves at school—try to keep as far out of it as possible, and leave their child to get on as best he may. Some worry far too much about small details, and so worry their child and make him nervous or stubborn according to his nature. Patience and understanding are needed on both sides. Over-anxious parents, especially of young children, are apt to try to talk to a teacher while she should be looking after her class, so that she only gives them half her attention and feels slightly irritated that they cannot see she has her hands full. Teachers, on the other hand, are apt to be on the defensive and resent as criticism of the school what is really lack of understanding, or maybe a badly expressed plea for help. Teachers need to know and to be able to explain to parents what they are trying to do for a child and why. This is not easy for a young teacher, because much of the work of an intelligent and well-trained teacher is at first intuitive. Small group discussions with parents, and prepared talks to parents on the work she is doing with the children in her class, teach her how to explain her work. A confident teacher who understands what she is doing is much the more able to accept criticism and use it where it is good or to understand and resolve the difficulty where the criticism is mistaken.

The old idea that schools and parents were best kept apart, is dying out. The unifying process began with the nursery classes and has crept up the school. Some teachers are still afraid of parents and think they will try to run the school. But parents are far too busy to want to do any such thing, and it is the business of a wise head to use to the utmost any parents who have time and talents to give, to help the school, either by serving on the school committee or in practical ways. Not only does the school get extra help, but an important bond is forged between the school (which is all too apt to become a closed community) and the outside world, and this enlarging of the atmosphere is good for staff as well as children. It is good for parents, too, in that the school is no longer a mere necessity, but an interest which they share with their children.

It is interesting that activity methods which at first sight appear individualistic—each child setting himself to the job nearest his own heart—are, in fact, a means of drawing together the whole class and of making connections between many subjects.

When a class of children have been working at their own interests, there comes a time when the room is tidied up and the children themselves report on what they have done. In this way they learn from each other's experience. They see where there are possibilities for two groups to join up in a larger project; they also see— sometimes of their own volition and sometimes because their teacher is there to guide their interest—how what they have done can lead on to a new and richer interest. For instance: a seven-year-old boy brought his Dinkie Aeroplane (a three-inch model) to school, and played with it with a friend. Next day several other boys brought toy planes. A group began to build hangars and an airfield. Other children had model cars but not aeroplanes, and so brought their cars and made little garages for them. In discussion of their play, they hit on the idea of combining the car and aeroplane groups in making and serving a model airfield. Meanwhile some more adventurous boys had stretched threads across and along the classroom so that the planes could be really airborne. This led to the need for more airfields, one at the end of each thread. At this point the teacher was called in to find real names for the airfields. Maps were studied (these children were already used to looking at motoring maps with their fathers). Airports were connected up at ground level by shipping and model railways. So from the bringing of a toy aeroplane to school this group work had developed showing the connectedness of various kinds of travel.

This kind of work causes real bringing together of studies, of interests and of children. It is a unifying process, and therefore enlarges their understanding and leads them to seek for fresh knowledge. In Froebel's words: "The most delightful and fruitful of all the intellectual energies is the perception of similarity and agreement by which we rise from the individual to the general and trace sameness in diversity, and master, instead of being mastered by, the multiplicity of nature."[1] Such unification must come from the children themselves. It is the business of the teacher to watch, and as often to create, situations where the children may make connections, but if she imposes her ready-made plans and unities on the children, the whole matter is often still-born. There was a period in Froebelian education about the first decade of this century when "correlation of subjects" was the watchword of Froebel teachers. Springing from the excellent idea of unity, this became in too many cases a mere rule-of-thumb method. It was possible to see children of six years begin the morning by singing a song about ducks; go on to do arithmetic about ducks, ducklings, duck eggs, etc.; study the "Ducks' Ditty" for poetry; copy out a verse of it for writing; model a duck's nest from plasticine (of all unsuitable media), and finish up with a story of the Ugly Duckling. In such an exaggerated—but true—example, it is easy to see that the teachers' imposed idea of unity left little room for the children themselves to make what Froebel called their own "inner connection". One has always to remember that a subject will arouse probably

[1] *The Education of Man.*

as many different connections as there are children in the class; but group feeling is likely to sway the majority of the children towards understanding one or two of the connections especially. A sensitive teacher is able to feel the way the interests of her class are going, and to foster by the material she provides, or the suggestions she makes, those interests which seem likely to be most productive.

Although part of Dr. Montessori's doctrine is unacceptable to Froebelians, they would agree that it was probably she rather than any other who put the child himself back in the centre of the educational picture, and made Froebel teachers realise how far they were straying from their own master in imposing a ready-made unity or correlation on their classes instead of fostering the children's own growth towards unity.

Correlation, projects, centres of interests, activities— all are attempts to use the energy that flows into his work when a child realises and uses the connection between one subject and another; each works as long as it is the interest of the children themselves that is leading the way, and is fostered by a wise teacher. Each becomes merely a dead system when imposed from without by a teacher who knows the letter but not the spirit of the law.

For the most part an interest will develop within a class and necessarily will become the special work of that class alone, as in a class play, a class magazine, a shop, a circus, an exhibition or a series of lectures by the children; but sometimes an interest which begins within a class brims over and embraces other classes. This gives rise not only to a broadening and deepening of the study, but, by helping children to work together with those who are not their usual workmates, it enlarges their understanding and appreciation of others. The "Oh, jolly good!" with which a surprised senior of twelve may greet the work of an eight-year-old not only gives confidence and incentive to the younger child, it also gives that increase in understanding to the senior which always comes with generous praise.

A class of children aged about eleven had—under their class mistress who was in charge of the school fiction library—organised a "Library Week". The aim was to inaugurate a new classification of the library which they had helped to carry out; to put on show the new books which a generous grant had bought; and to urge readers to a greater interest in, and care of, library books. They asked each form that was of an age to do so, to make a large sheet with writing and pictures on the life and works of one author. This led to some profitable work in all the classes from the nine-year-olds upwards; and some interesting sheets on R. L. S., Kenneth Grahame, Lewis Carroll, etc., were produced. The readings at school assembly that week were chosen and read by the children of the organising class to fit in with the interest of the week. There was a book quiz competition, with book-tally prizes. Parents and friends of the school were invited to see the exhibition set out in the school entrance hall, and for a week at least the whole of the upper school was united in many common interests, and found great pleasure in studying the exhibits of bindings, printing and dust covers, as well as each other's sheets of work on authors. This piece of work was first thought of by the teacher, partly because she was head librarian and partly because the National Libraries were at that time celebrating their centenary. In this case the interest of the children was of her cultivation, but she took time to study her class, prepare the ground, plant the seeds, and so reaped a harvest of interest which was very real because it was something for which the class was ready. They were rather a backward class, with a low opinion of themselves and their capabilities. They would not on their own initiative have considered themselves capable of organising an exhibition for the whole school, but as they were encouraged and led forward, their own ideas began to flow, and the general admiration for the exhibition had an excellent effect on the morale of the class. The previous year they had been notably lacking in literary taste, but now—partly because from re-cataloguing the library they knew better what was there, and partly because the exhibition had given them a good opinion of themselves—they began to read for pleasure far more widely and wisely.

The form mistress, a month or two after the exhibition, opened her room one night a week to any boarders who liked to form a reading circle. This was greatly appreciated by her own form. As one girl of twelve remarked: "It's so nice to get a little peace to read." It was also noticed that these same children on other evenings were obviously finding great joy in reading, whereas formerly they had been playing "horses" or tending their mice all the time. The interest in reading and the fact that they were reading books which they could talk about to their parents led to a new "connection"; for whereas in many cases the parents of this particular set had only been able to remark the bad spelling and general backwardness of their daughters, they now found they were able to share with them the delights of *Lorna Doone*, *Uncle Tom's Cabin* and *The Children of the New Forest*. Thus a new and happy connection was made between parents and children, which was especially important to girls who needed to have their self-confidence built up.

Another example of an interest which would not have grown without the foresight and skill of a teacher was the Bach Festival Week. In this case the ground had been prepared over years by the growing up of a voluntary school choir, by the interest of the children in their music lessons on the life and works of Bach and by the work of the school orchestra. With all these ingredients, it was but necessary for the senior children to be told that the world was celebrating the bi-centenary of the great master and the work of holding a school festival was set afoot. In this case school assembly and concerts became focal-points; but they were backed up by an exhibition of relevant books and pictures. In a case like this, once the interest is aroused, staff and children work together for an end which both understand and desire. This seems the best sort of education that a school can achieve. Children and teachers combine in new and hitherto un-suspected ways, parents too may be called in to contri-bute to the music, and the children once more carry home interests which cause their parents to realise with pleasure a new bond that they may forge with a maturing son or daughter.

The most obvious heritage to the school of this festival week was a series of Bach hymns which raised the musical level of school assembly considerably. What was less easy to assess but still more valuable was the increase in musical appreciation. A ten-year-old boarder startled her mother by saying, "I like Bach best of all the musi-cians." When asked why, she replied by humming various of his phrases and melodies and saying, "That's the sort of thing I like about him."

We have been discussing here two sorts of unity or connection which intermingle. There is first the intel-lectual unity, the connecting of various subjects in the mind of the student. This, in the early days especially, we shall best foster by watching for the interests which spring naturally from the children, and seeing how we can lead these on by showing where new materials or new skills may be used, or by providing in the children's environment something which will open their eyes to new possibilities. Though a teacher must beware of dragging the children so fast that they cannot really follow (in which case their interest flags and the work falls dead),

yet it is her work to foresee possible development, and by
her sympathy with her class to lead them always to a
widening and deepening of their own real interests. By
this means the class will inevitably find their real need for
skill in reading and writing and even in elementary arithmetic. Once the connection with these skills is made and
the need for them fully realised, it is the responsibility of
the teacher to see that the children give enough time to
practise these (to them) long and arduous studies. A
young child cannot take a sufficiently long view to
realise that the days and years of toil in these subjects
are going to bring him an adequate recompense. Therefore the teacher, by art, must provide short-term incentives to study, and the best of all these incentives is the
sense of mastery which comes when a child is doing work
graded to suit his capability. She will also see that his
time is rightly divided between following his real
interests and the study of tool subjects, without which his
interests can never develop very far.

The older the children grow the more do they become
conscious members of a group swayed by group interests,
and the more safely can a teacher put her suggestions
before the class. The children are still suggestible, and
unwise adult interference can still kill an interest either
by carrying it on to lines alien to the class or by going
faster than the class can follow; but because children of
nine can discuss their ideas more clearly and judge the
teacher's suggestions with some understanding, the
sympathetic teacher can increasingly join in the planning
of interests and projects as her class grows older; and
should be able to do this without lifting the feeling of
responsibility for the work from her class.

The air-travel work of the seven-year-old class, which
led on in such a lively way to reading and writing and
geography of travel, sprang directly from the interest of
two boys in their toy aeroplanes and the desire to play

with them. It became a valuable part of the school work because it was fostered by a teacher always on the watch for opportunity.

The Library Week and the Bach Festival were, on the other hand, ideas induced by teachers, but they were seeds that fell into well-prepared ground and took root so that the children came to regard them as their own projects and gained both responsibility and pleasure from them. The opportunity for guidance increases as the children mature.

The second kind of unity mentioned here is the unity between people which comes from this type of work. It hardly needs to be pointed out that training in critical appreciation of the work of others, which means understanding their capabilities, talents and weaknesses, co-operating with them, helping them, learning from them, is of paramount importance in training men and women to take their right places in the world. Competition probably has its uses: it is within limitations great fun to compete for prizes even if those prizes be only marks and honours; it may occasionally stimulate a clever child to do a better piece of work than he would have done otherwise, but the true disciple of Froebel can never allow that competition should be the real incentive to work, since it is ultimately a dividing and disruptive force. Teachers themselves know well enough that marks cannot make the dull boy quick—they merely underline his dullness till, seeing his name week by week at the bottom of the list, he lapses into apathy or despair, while the clever boy often keeps at the top of the list with little trouble. A few intelligent children whose taste has already been impaired by unwise offers of fortuitous rewards may work a little harder than they would have done to gain a high place on the mark list, but any good to them is usually offset by the anxiety of the duller children, who, as every teacher knows, are often so obsessed by the desire to please their parents by gaining good marks that they cannot attend to their work at all from sheer anxiety. Effort, which is the one thing a good teacher wishes to mark, cannot be marked on a list without making a travesty of the whole thing from the point of view of the class.

Reward and punishment seem to be part of the make-up of life. A good piece of work or good effort is to some extent its own reward, but for young children especially it needs to be underlined by the approbation of the teacher. Work badly done brings a rebuke, or must be done again. It is a mistake to think that a school which has no marks has no standards either. Remarks take the place of marks, and by far the most efficient correction takes place when the teacher is able to correct the work with the child, rather than score it with red ink corrections (which a child rarely reads). In a sense children will compete for good remarks, and there may be special competitions in which special—often out-of-school effort —is rewarded with a prize. End-of-term examinations bring at least their "pass" or "fail", and often a graded mark list. Such occasional competition appears to be stimulating, and gives a child who tries some opportunity of finding out about his powers without having the prolonged bad effect of the weekly mark list. Above all, by casting off the burden of general school marks, the way is made clear for co-operation, for group work and for valuing also those subjects (usually the more ethical ones) which cannot be marked as arithmetic, spelling and other skills can be marked. Some hold that lazy children need the constant stimulation of marks, but a Froebel school is dealing usually with young children who should not have had time to form habits of laziness. A lazy *young* child is almost always more or less ill— physically, mentally or spiritually—and such illness needs a cure that goes deeper than competition. The normal child works because of an intense inner urge to grow up, to find out and to know, and the school is there to canalise his energy into channels which have been found most useful to society and the individual in general.

Since, when he grows up, the good citizen will join himself with others to continue his search for the good, true and beautiful, it seems right that from his earliest days he should learn to regard this search as something right and delightful in which he is united with others, and not as a lonely grind in competition against all the rest.

In sections 8 and 9 of *The Education of Man*, Froebel discusses the treatment of those children the wholeness of whose inner life has already been marred. For these children he says: "Directly categorical, mandatory education in its full severity is demanded." But, he continues: "We cannot tell at first how greatly the inner life of the child has been permanently damaged; at least we cannot tell until the advent of intelligent self-consciousness, of unity in life between God and man, of establishing harmony and community in life between father and son, disciple and master." Therefore until this time, that is adolescence, the school and his parents must try to adapt his surroundings to his needs, to let them make his failings clear to him, affording him the minimum of opportunities for injury from the outbreaks and consequences of his inner failings, and the maximum of pleasure from the right use of his healthy and good characteristics.

Froebel himself was an experienced teacher. He knew that children never reach school age quite perfect; but he was a practical idealist and knew how a little child who comes amongst others, spoilt or timid and insecure, passionate or obstinate, is often not so deeply marked as would appear from the outward behaviour, and in general the life of the nursery or kindergarten, or even of an older class, will of itself check the hurt and allow

the good to develop. In this case, too, the power of the
natural desire for unity is drawing the child towards
health; for bad behaviour naturally excludes him from
the companionship he consciously or unconsciously longs
for. The part of the teacher at this stage is rarely that of
retribution and justice, but rather of a loving watcher
who can help to rescue him from the clutches of an old
bad habit or an emotion he can no longer master alone.
She can show him the way out of his frustration and despair. She, when his passion wants to harm someone else,
is as a wall to shut him off and prevent him, till the fit is
gone. It is better known now than in Froebel's day that
children may be terrified by the evil passions they feel
within them, and they often stand in dire need of all the
strength a teacher has to protect them from themselves.
Hence the sense of repose one often finds in a preparatory
class where the teacher, though kind, is stern; and where
children know they will not be allowed to misbehave.
Too much stern rule means, of course, too little training
in self-discipline; but in the early stages it is most important that children shall feel the protective power of the
teacher to help them to "be good"—that is, to help them
to feel a happy contributing part of the whole group.

Protection from evil, however, is not enough. Children
will not grow properly without love and approbation.

Froebel writes sternly of the harm done by parents and
teachers "who first make the child or boy bad—by
attributing evil—or at least wrong motives to all that a
child does from ignorance, precipitation or even from a
keen and praiseworthy sense of right and wrong. Such
birds of ill omen are the first to bring guilt upon such a
child, who, though not wholly innocent is yet without
guilt, for they give him motives and incentives which
were as yet unknown to him, they make his actions bad,
though not, at first, his will; they kill him spiritually. . . .
They act like the good-natured little boy who says of his

fly or beetle, that is weak from maltreatment, or has even lost its feet, 'See, how tame!' " [1]

Froebel hotly denies the original depravity of man. Belief in it is a blasphemy against God, and he holds that "the only infallible remedy for counteracting any short-coming and even wickedness is to find the originally good side of the human being, that has been repressed, disturbed or misled into the shortcoming, and then foster, build up and properly guide this good side. Thus the shortcoming will at last disappear, though it may involve a hard struggle against habit, but not against original depravity in man". [2]

It is interesting to notice that the child whom today we call "the disturbed child" (whose "inner life is marred" in Froebel's words) feels cut off, and his naughtiness again and again takes the form of trying to find out how he stands with the group. Sometimes he attacks other children, sometimes he plays for attention in other ways; sometimes he steals or tries by some means to get power over others; but always he is concerned to find his way back into the community which he believes has rejected him and whose overtures he is often too fearful to see or understand. In a formal school, where each child works as an entity in himself, such a child does not recognise his feelings of being outcast so keenly. In a Froebel class where there is more emphasis on co-operation and unity, he is liable to feel his isolation more and react with greater violence, but at least in this case the trouble is on the surface and can be dealt with, and there is less danger of driving underground a wrong attitude to life.

Froebel found in story-telling a means of connecting work done in the kindergarten with life outside. When the four-year-olds had been building with their little blocks—walls, chairs, steps, houses—the teacher was to

---

[1] *The Education of Man*, section 51.
[2] *Ibid.*, section 52.

tell them a story, bringing in all these objects that they had themselves built, so that the children might have their activity enriched by greater imaginative understanding, and a feeling that all is bound up in living. Today our children's play is informal. We no longer demand that all shall build at one moment. What was freedom a hundred years ago would seem slavish and meaningless today; but we still believe in the value of stories, and still seek by means of them both to interpret the children to themselves and to carry their experience farther and farther beyond the walls of home and school. It is a delight to see the appreciation which children of five have for the story called: "Milly Molly Mandy locked in." This is about a fear so many of them have known. Their pleasure when the young heroine takes her trouble philosophically and makes the best of it, their relief when at last her father lets her out, all show how keenly they identify themselves with her. The parable of the lost sheep has the same sort of appeal. Not only are their troubles and fears interpreted, but they are gaining the idea of kinship, of unity with others who have feelings like their own.

As the children grow older stories lead them ever farther and farther afield to share experiences and emotions of others. Froebel would have children from the earliest infancy learn the dignity of human labour. In his *Mother Songs*, and later in verses and stories, he wants children to hear of the simple people and those who provide for our daily needs, just as—with the same end in view—he wishes children to help their parents in home and workshop that they may feel themselves as useful and responsible members of their own community.

As girls and boys reach the hero-worship stage, the stories must provide material for their minds to work upon, but the value of stories in education is now so widely accepted that there is little need to stress it here.

III

So far I have tried to show how important to the school of today are two of Froebel's ideas, first of self-activity, which gives power to learn and to concentrate, and secondly of connectedness, which leads children to seek that fundamental satisfaction of our need for unity with nature, man and God.

These two ideas may well be held to embrace all the rest, but perhaps something more should be said of two aspects of activity which are especially obvious in schools.

First there is the "creativeness or expressive activity to produce assimilation of knowledge, growth of power and acquisition of skill". If the impression has been given that children in a Froebel school can escape all drudgery and practice work, this is far from the truth. Interesting work can be implemented with the older children only when they know how to study and have skill sufficient to write and read around the subject in hand. It is true that the group interest creates a need for the skill, and the practice of the skill makes the interest possible. Froebel was very clear that a child did not make a piece of work his own until he had in some way been active about it. This has already been noted in discussing creative activity. All teachers must know the disappointment of finding that a class has completely forgotten a story to which they listened, wrapt, a few months before. The truth seems to be that we make nothing our very own without some sort of toil.

This idea led to a terrible custom at one time when, after every story, poem or nature lesson, the children were called upon to express themselves in drawing, modelling or writing. The idea was good, but it was done to death. Some stories lend themselves to obvious and immediate illustration, others (and this is usually true also of poems) need to be thought over and assimilated before a child can draw or write about them. The teacher who follows Froebel will, however, remember that what comes out of the child is of paramount importance, since it tends to fix for him the impression he has received. She therefore sees to it that along with the learning and taking in, children have plenty of time to write, draw, paint, act or express in some way the ideas they are gaining; though she will not necessarily expect an immediate response to information or ideas given; and at times she must be content to hope she has sown a seed, though it may not germinate till years later.

The effect of Froebel's approach to formal subjects is perhaps seen best of all in mathematics, so often a mysterious bugbear to children. To the child in a Froebel school, numbers should have meaning. They are friends. He has used them in his games and occupations. He has measured himself and his friends. He has weighed out commodities in his shop games, he has measured water into pint, quart and gallon measures, long before he ever thought of these things as "sums".

Sums begin as records of what he has found out, and so arithmetic progresses as a more and more fascinating and complicated way of recording certain discoveries about numbers, shapes and sizes. The child who is not allowed to learn beyond what he can understand is safe to enjoy mathematics. The child who may get into difficulties is the one who has been away and missed the explanation of a new process or problem. The exact studies, like mathematics and language, call for the greatest vigilance on the part of teachers to see that children do not through absence miss out a vital step. It is this which is the cause of so much trouble and difficulty with arithmetic, French and Latin. Where these subjects are built up carefully, step by step, children enjoy them, both for themselves and because of the sense of power that comes from the mastery of something a little difficult.

Froebel's "gifts" were a wonderful piece of apparatus by which to teach mathematical truths, but like many another method, in the hands of dullards they were used dully and all the life went from them. But their lesson to the teacher still remains. Children need to see, to feel, to touch, to discover mathematical truths before they embark on any written exercises thereon.

Mathematics, like nature study, should be for children a discovery subject, not learning by rote without intelligence the findings of others. This does not mean there is no place for rote learning, but that a child needs to build up and know the meaning of multiplication tables, for instance, before he learns them by heart, so that he will learn and understand them for ever.

IV

Since the child to be educated consists of body as well as of mind and spirit, the school's business is with physical as well as with mental and spiritual development. More and more the three kinds of education overlap. "Music and movement" is education for body and spirit and mind; dancing requires memory and concentration as well as physical grace. Games demand physical discipline and training as well as fine moral qualities; swimming gives courage and poise. The advance in physical education during the last decades has been most encouraging. The study of the needs of children of different ages and how best to fulfil these by means of physical work is inspiring to watch. A few of the old singing games remain with us; not so much for any physical value as because of their traditional rightness for young children, and in some cases because of their dealing with such basic interests as farming and impersonation of animals. For the most part, however, they have been supplanted by freer and more energetic exercise. Yet Froebel, who encouraged his boys in all manly sports, who let them climb trees or ramble through the forest, or even go on camping expeditions, would surely enjoy the jungle-gyms, the scramble nets and all the other apparatus of today; and he who gave the ball as a first "gift" to a baby would delight in a playground full of children each with a ball gaily practising to gain the greatest measure of skill possible to each. He would be surprised, no doubt, at the lack of teachers and directors, since in his time each group of ten children had a director; but the freedom and self-direction of modern physical education would, after the first startled moment, give him pleasure, since it keeps the spirit if not the letter of his method.

Again Dr. Montessori recalled Froebel teachers to the true way when she showed how children should help to serve their own meals. Froebel himself pointed out how the young child loves to help in all practical ways, and how the child who is not allowed to help when he is very young seldom wants to help when he is older. To help to serve mid-morning lunch or even dinner is for a child of four not only a training in moving skilfully and carefully, it also teaches him something of the joys and responsibilities of service. Physical activity should not be limited to certain periods of the day. Our young adolescents all too frequently slouch and crouch when standing or sitting. No doubt this is partly due to fatigue at a time when they are growing fast, but much of it could be checked if teachers were more conscious of the importance of seeing that children sit and stand and move well all through their school life.

V

Finally Froebel demanded for children "happy and harmonious surroundings in which to grow". Thanks largely to the work of psychologists, it is now widely realised that children need an atmosphere of love and peace to give them poise and a feeling of security. But often through lack of thought, realisation lags far behind theory in this matter. The anxiety or bickering of parents is often cited as cause for some behaviour difficulty in a child. It is not so often realised that tension and worry in members of a school staff also react on the children, and differences between school and parents raise conflicting loyalties, which are hard for children to bear.

The inspector of the Keilhau School wrote of Froebel himself:

"He has bound to himself in brotherliness and friendship his fellow workers, as the supports and pillars of his life work, which to him truly is holy work. That this union, this brotherhood so to speak, among the teachers, must have the most salutary influence on the instruction and training, and on the pupils themselves, is self-evident."

The inspector goes on to report the domestic order he found throughout the school, and noted with pleasure the punctuality and cleanliness so unusual in a school of those days. To Froebel these things mattered because he was dealing with the whole of life. The idea has now gone far and wide, and the attempt to bring harmony and grace into all school life is no longer limited to Froebel schools, though emergency conditions still force some to scrambled ugly meal-times and dingy classrooms.

Where ugly surroundings must—for a while at least—be endured, flowers and pictures may bring their own beauty. Though many schools for young children are still housed in dreary buildings, we can in some schools at least see how light and air and fair outlook may make a schoolroom a joyous place. But however beautiful or dreary the classroom may be, all children need the opportunity at times to go on expeditions to see and study the outside world as a part of their education.

Froebel's school was situated in the forest, and happy are those schools which, like his, are situated so that children can wander near by in the natural beauty of the country-side, play and experiment in a real stream, and test their courage by climbing real trees. Happy are those who, looking back on their school-days, remember not scarred desks and benches only, but the beauty of a tree in spring in the school garden, the wonder of a dragonfly emerging from his larva case in the classroom aquarium, a sunset behind the elms of the playing-fields, or the scent of the lilac floating in at the window on a drowsy May afternoon.

We cannot foretell what a child will remember—a chance remark, a momentary expression, a fleeting moment of beauty—or of terror. We do know, however, that consciously or unconsciously he will carry away from school impressions that the world is a good or bad place to be in, and these impressions will largely condition the mood in which he will go forth to meet life.

Froebel would have us send a child forth active, not passive, having kept that delight in giving which is so characteristic of young children; "he would have him grow towards a state where he is clear concerning himself and in himself, growing in peace with nature towards union with God" (Bowen).

The Baroness von Marenholtz-Bülow, one of Froebel's greatest disciples, wrote:

"All work, all exercises, which awaken the active powers which form the capacity for rendering loving services to fellow creatures, will help to lay the ground work of religion in the child. The awakening of love goes before that of faith . . . but love must show itself in deeds, and this will be impossible unless there be ability to do. A child can no more be educated to a life of religion and faith without the exercise of personal activity than heroic deeds can be accomplished by words only."

Our schools, then, must be busy, active places; there will be difficulties, quarrels, lessons to be learnt again and again, punishments as well as rewards. There will be shouting and laughter, and quiet moments for reading or watching; most of all perhaps we hope that those moments when teacher and children watch together the miracles of nature will remain an experience for life.

In school we have tried to equip them for life; to meet difficulties bravely, to prepare them to be "free thinking independent men". As they go forth—aged ten, twelve or fourteen—to the larger world of the secondary school, what strength, we wonder, do they carry in themselves. Have we, as we hope, begun to develop within them that threefold harmony of body, mind and spirit which is the basis for the good life?

CHAPTER V

THE RELIGIOUS ROOTS OF
FROEBEL'S PHILOSOPHY

FROEBEL'S approach to education is a religious one, and his religion, in spirit and in language, is Christian. His opportunity to teach seemed to him in retrospect a religious vocation, and the circumstances in which it came to show the working of "a good Providence". It is not possible to discuss his philosophy of education without conceding that in his own mind its source and its vindication came from his religious belief. He affirms it explicitly and vigorously in his definitions of purpose and his descriptions of method. He implies it consistently as he describes the field of educational activity. "Education as a whole . . . will bring to man's consciousness and render efficient in his life the fact that man and nature proceed from God and are conditioned by Him—that both have their being in God. . . . Therefore the school should first of all teach the religion of Christ; therefore it should first of all, and above all, give instruction in the Christian religion; everywhere and in all zones the school should instruct for and in this religion."

There is no escape from the force of this language nor from its organic relation to his whole exposition. A knowledge of the nature of God and of man's essential unity with God was to him the necessary way of man's fulfilment of his destiny. This unity of man with God was the source of that total unity which Froebel believed he had come to know in his relations with nature, with society and in his experience of life. This unity was to be the goal of education. "The truth of this conviction about the Christian religion is the sole foundation of all insight and knowledge." His claims for it are remarkable. It made genuine human education truly possible, and alone gave meaning and purpose to life. Therefore when he is speaking of the curriculum, he speaks of the primacy of religious knowledge, and sets a nature study which is approached in an essentially religious spirit immediately second. "Only the Christian, only the human being with Christian spirit . . . can possibly attain a true understanding and a living knowledge of nature." When he speaks of the function of parents in education, it is to remind them of their inescapable responsibility to live with their children in such a relationship as may yield faith in the Fatherhood of God. When he describes the nature of the school, it is to suggest that it should be the kind of community which exemplifies those laws of love which are the nature of God.

It is perhaps this peculiar quality of the religious genius of Froebel that his enthusiasm for a religious approach to education does not lead him into the excesses of dogmatic instructions. In part his insight into the nature of the child would not allow this; in part, it must be admitted, it was due to his own undogmatic approach to the Christian faith. His religious opinions were indeed highly individualistic; there is little formal theology behind them, any more than there is any consistent philosophical pattern to his thought. His thinking seems to be largely the rationalising of an attitude which proceeded from experiences which were the deep source of personal faith and educational purpose alike. He would seem to have accepted such ideas from the philosophical thought of his time as qualify that experience, and to have resisted such thought as did not comply with it. From Schelling, for example, may well have come the idea that the unity in the nature of the world is found in a force which is not mechanical but an eternal process of self-activity. He certainly agreed with Krause that there was an analogy between the organic development of nature and life in the spiritual world. But it is clear from his *Autobiography* that the direction of his religious thinking came from other and more personal sources. The unhappiness of his relation to the father to whom he was "a stranger for life", and a stepmother who began by being indifferent and continued by misjudging and ill-treating him, turned him in upon himself, "to study my own consciousness". There he retreated from the formal pattern of religious ideas and the drastic religious judgments of his preaching father. Relieved that he was not destined to go to Hell, he found in the quiet observation of nature a power of comfort, and what is more, an evidence of other and more reassuring spiritual relations. The good uncle, also a parson, who came into his life at this time of emancipation, confirmed the young Froebel's desire to believe that there was another and kindlier way of knowing God, and gave it a positive Christian sanction through his own gracious love and the warm and friendly accent of his preaching. Under such a kindly sky, Froebel's idealism flowered. His nature, which badly needed the love he had found in his uncle's home, easily fused the genial aspect of the Christian Father God, of whom he now heard so much, with the thoughts about "natural law in the spiritual world" which had come to him in his communings with nature.

This gave his thinking an unquestioned direction, which remains consistent throughout all the development of his educational theory. Here is a mind disposed to be philosophical without a training in the disciplines of philosophy, which is remarkable rather for its insights than for its logic. The opposition of the Church to his "heresies" did not shake him. The spring of his personal faith rose from deeper levels. His mind, which could not suffer set forms, could well discern the authority of those experiences in which he lived and worked. It remains

Making Puppets out of Newspaper

as hard to defend the orthodoxy of his Christian belief
as to deny the decisive influence of the personal religious
experience of a man who wrote "man needs to be educated for the everlasting here and beyond of each new
moment of existence, for the everlasting rest, everlasting
activity and everlasting life in God".

Froebel's idea of the nature of God derives from his interpretation of the work of God as he has known it in his
own experience and interpreted it in the life of nature.
God is the absolute unity and the spirit which moves in
man to seek that unity in his own life, in his relation with
his fellows and in his relation with nature. It is His nature
and desire to reveal Himself; this He does through His
creative energy, and we can know Him in part in so far
as we become godlike through our own creative activity.
He has manifested Himself in and through a man "who
absorbed His whole being in himself, and was therefore
His Son", through whom we are able to know our own
sonship. He makes Himself known also through the
pressure of His spirit seeking unity in us and through us.
Yet when Froebel says that the revelation of the one self-
existent Being of God must from its very nature be
triune, he does not mean what the Christian theologian
means by the doctrine of the Trinity; his Trinity is more
a description of the way man experiences God than of the
nature of God Himself. He makes no secret of his dependence upon nature for his experience of God. The processes of nature, as it were, symbolise the life of the spirit
of trust in God and obedience to Him. In the mystery of
growth from within, "slowly and silently performed",
Froebel sees a parable of the child's religious development. In his sense of the inevitability of such growth
where the conditions are good, he echoes the particular
parables of Jesus which he specially admires. Froebel
indeed finds no difficulty in going further: the order and
care he thinks he observes in external nature seem to him

evidences of the activity of a spirit the child can know in the care and order of his own life. He even claims "that the pure spirit of God not only is seen more clearly and distinctly in nature than it is in human life, but in the clear disclosures of God's spirit in nature are seen the nature, dignity and holiness of man reflected in all their pristine clearness and purity."

These words sound odd today; they apparently mean that the same spirit of God in his Unity must be at work in His whole creation, in nature as in Man. Man may therefore see in nature, if he will, an undistorted evidence of the quality of life he should know and enjoy himself. To say no more, Froebel would seem to be selective and partial in his conception of nature. His approach is that of the man who has learned how to contemplate but has chosen to look only at what he wanted to see. There is no suspicion even of nature's indifference to man's welfare; no hint of nature as being a cause of suffering in man, both in body and in mind. One looks in vain for any sense of the ageless struggle of man with the earth or with the sea, or of the endless conflict with nature in which man seems to be locked. The approach is that of the contemplative artist and not the scientist or even the theologian. Only in a benign setting can Froebel have been content with such a view of man's relation to nature. There is no more need to doubt the integrity of the experience of unity with nature or the wisdom of the lessons to be learned from subduing ourselves to the great rhythms of the natural order or from humbling ourselves before the mystery of growth than to doubt that Wordsworth did feel "a presence which disturbed me with the joy of elemental thoughts". Aldous Huxley's witty essay on *Wordsworth in the Tropics* (with its ironical description of the discomforts and dilemmas of the contemplative life in the jungle) exposed a conception of nature as selective and as partially true as Froebel's. Froebel's

position is, however, consistent with the rest of his thinking and his conviction that God, the Creator Artist of the
universe, can be known in His creation is unshakable. At
this point one cannot but feel that he is nearer to pan-
theism than Christian thinking, even though he claims
that only a Christian can so see God in nature.

Froebel is nearer the Christian position when he
describes the relation of a son to a father. He affirms that
there is no form of unity so complete and satisfying as
such a relationship springing from dependence and care,
shared purpose and mutual understanding. He counts
the enjoyment of such a relation in the home to be the
greatest privilege of a child and the greatest responsibility of a parent. His experience as an adopted son in his
uncle's home and his interpretation of the relationship of
Jesus Christ to His father were, no doubt, the source of
this belief. Man, he says in effect, can recognise God as
his Father if he recognises his inner self to be from God
and therefore to be dependent upon Him. To know this
is to be at one with God and to be at peace. If in addition
man accepts this relation in obedience as the necessity
and freedom of his daily life, then he discovers the true
unity and purpose of his being. It is the work primarily
of the parent, but also of the teacher, to offer to a child
such a "spiritually human relation" and to help him to
interpret it clearly as in very truth an experience of God.
Froebel is quite specific about these responsibilities. He
details a method for training the child in simple piety,
and shows the great value of the acts of prayer which a
mother can lead and of the words which a mother can
make lovingly familiar. He shows how the concept of
father can be filled with happy and trustful associations
by parents, and how Christian values can be best learned
as they are encountered in the child's experience of his
parents' understanding, their patience and their forgive-
ness. He has anticipated the recognition in our day that

one of the decisive influences in Christian education is the quality of the love between the father and mother, and their willingness to acknowledge that as the gift of God to them. He might not have said as sharply as Agatha in *The Family Reunion*: "I think that the things that are taken for granted at home make a deeper impression upon children than what they are told"; but he had sensed that it was true, and hoped that the fact of God as Love might be the great assumption of family education.

The Work of Christ

What part the life and work of Jesus Christ play in the development of Froebel's thought it is difficult to say. His early experience in two different ministerial homes had, no doubt, led him to accept the place of Jesus as central to the Christian faith. As he outlines the growth of his position, however, the figure of Jesus is rather a confirming authority than the Way by which man comes to God. It was not perhaps all gain that the softer colours of his uncle's portrait of Jesus blurred the severer lines of the figure about whom his father preached. It is perhaps not altogether strange that it is possible for Froebel to discuss the revelation which God made to man in Jesus Christ without so much as a mention of the Cross or the Resurrection. What we do find is an insight into the filial relation of Jesus to God, which suggests that to Froebel this was the unique value of his life. He even interprets the uniqueness of "the only begotten son" by saying that God found a man who "absorbed His whole being in himself and who was *therefore* His son". This Jesus would seem rather to have arrived than to have been sent, but as Froebel saw him he had certainly arrived at an intimate unity with God which illuminated for all men the nature of their own life. This Jesus is an archetype of the son in every man; he is the supreme observer who saw in nature and in man the life of God, and he found his fulfilment, as must every man, in dependence and in obedience. The sayings of Jesus are assumed as the truth about human relationships, and men are bidden to behold his life and works. Jesus is "our highest ideal", in which he says we recognise the voice of God.

It is natural that such a conception of the work of Jesus involves Froebel in an attitude to the Christian life which suggests that man, too, must "arrive". The Christian religion is "the eternal conviction of the truth of the teachings of Jesus and a firm persistent conduct in obedience to this conviction". To this conviction and to this persistence man has, however, to raise himself. He even seems to have believed that it was not impossible for man to live the life of Jesus in its purity, and to show it forth to the world. This whole view depends upon Froebel's optimistic view of the nature of man and a highly selective choice of the sayings of Jesus; he has not focused his gaze upon the Gospel's picture of one sent to seek and save that which was lost, nor explored the consciousness of one who believed that he had something to do for man that man could not do for himself if he was to reconcile him to God. His Christ may be illumination, but he is not power. This Christ does, however, exactly what needs to be done in Froebel's thinking; he does confirm that central position of man in the universe, and shows the nature of man's kinship with God which is the foundation of Froebel's whole system of education. He certainly recognised in Jesus a mind in deepest sympathy with his own about the nature of teaching. He recognises how reluctant Jesus was to impose formal categorical teaching upon minds unready or unwilling for it. He accepts gratefully the refusal of Jesus to impose pattern or example upon them, and finds the anticipation of his own oneness with God in nature in the teaching of Our Lord about growing things. What he has

left out is the conflict in the soul of Jesus and the passion
for men which went to the Cross.

The Nature of Man

Froebel believed invincibly in the divinity of man; he
derived this faith from his conception of the unity of God's
creation. "Every human being should be viewed and
treated as a manifestation of the divine spirit in human
form." It was blasphemous indeed to think of man's
nature as other than good; it cannot even be neutral,
neither good nor bad in itself: if it is the creation of God,
it must be good. What is evil, and Froebel does not of
course deny that the behaviour of children can quite
early be wilful and stubborn, comes either from the un-
balanced development of the child's nature or, more
likely, from forceful, unimaginative treatment. If the
child's nature is set free from unnatural restraints (shades
of another prison house), he will grow by the light of his
own nature into a vision of his unity with God and man.
This is Rousseau with a Christian interpretation. Froebel
is quite precise in his description of the causes of wayward
and wilful behaviour in children; it begins, he says, when
they are denied the attention they have the right to expect; they develop a sense of guilt when it is imputed to
them, probably by the Church. About no one does Froebel
talk with more vehemence than about ill-informed and
misguided teachers and pastors. Certainly the one place
from which evil does not originate is the child's own
nature. Set him in the right environment in a loving
home with teachers who understand how to encourage
growth but not to force it, in a place where he can respond
to the simplicities of nature and enjoy the companionship of like-minded boys and girls, and he will surely
come to a knowledge of his own nature as a child of God
and to his oneness with his fellows.

The achievement of wisdom is the highest aim of man,

and so, conversely, the origin of all evil is falsehood; not that falsehood has a real existence, it is only the perversion of the good by error in thinking. So every manifestation which seems to be evil is, in fact, a contradiction of something that is good. One of the highest functions of the educator is therefore to reveal the true source of the perverted impulse and to allow the original good to find a new direction. This discovery or enlightenment is what Froebel would mean by conversion. He concedes that at this point of change the man may well have a hard struggle against the power of habit, but by self-active application of knowledge in an educating environment man can recover his true destiny. He will have nothing of original depravity or original sin. As in his view of nature and of the person of Jesus, so in his thought about man, the element of conflict seems understressed. Strangely, Froebel's theory of opposites did not seem to him to demand a reality of evil as the condition of the reality of good. His central conviction that man is the child of God seemed to him to be threatened by any admission of the possibility that man bears a personal responsibility for the choice of evil rather than good. What he says positively about the nature of man and his need of release would come much more urgently if he had been more aware of the conflict within and without our human nature and the offer that the Christian religion makes to resolve it. To know the good does not necessarily imply the power to achieve the good, and to be released from ignorance or falsehood is not sufficient to sustain the desire for truth.

What Emerges?

Nevertheless, something vital for our educational thinking today emerges from a consideration of Froebel's religious outlook. No one has seen more clearly that education needs a purpose beyond itself. He knew for what he was educating children, and it was nothing less than total unity within the person and with other persons and with God. If a person is to grow he must know what he is growing into, and his growth must be in his widening and deepening relationships. It would not be sufficient for Froebel if men were to be educated for personal fulfilment in itself, nor for the service of the community or state in itself; neither the individual nor the community are ends in themselves save as they find their life and purpose in God. His sense of the ultimate unity which is to be known and enjoyed is vital and irreplaceable. The fact that we may feel he achieved this unity too easily by leaving out inconvenient and contradictory phenomena does not diminish the urgency of his concern. Those who are indebted to him for his vision of education have to see today, in the light of it, how to present this truly religious purpose in full view of all the facts. Psychology has taught us more about the origins of love and hate, the sources of good and evil, and helped us to understand the conflicts in human nature; sociology has shown us more about the influences that create and destroy the true life of a community; Christian theology is recovering from idealism and a misguided view of the inevitability of progress, and is presenting more strongly a view of God who has taken the initiative in dealing with the sources and power of evil. Standing at any one or at all of these points, we are today compelled to see a unity which is more truly a reconciliation and a synthesis. A true unity must comprehend the whole, and only such can be a worthy foundation for a philosophy of education. We are being constrained to consider more seriously, in other words, that true education must be "religious". At this point again Froebel has something of primary value to say to us; he will not have it that the need for religious experience involves the pressure of formal patterns of thought, conduct or belief prematurely upon the growing child. Our very sense of need for a

more ordered and complete statement of religious faith
may make this peril even greater than it was in Froebel's
time. Political or religious ideologies alike threaten where
they seek to serve. Froebel will call the educators of this
time, and especially the Christian educators, to remember
the conditions under which integrity and sincerity can
be achieved. He will not allow us to take refuge in a
barren neutrality; he knows that we cannot avoid the
responsibility for positive influence. What he does say is
first of all to parents to remind them of the responsibility
of those who first give the child a view of what his wider
relationships can be. It is perhaps more true today than
Froebel can have known that the sources of trust in man
and confidence in God lie in the security of family love.
Teachers, and especially Christian teachers (it is difficult
to imagine what Froebel would have thought of religious
"specialists"), are reminded of their responsibility to
interpret experience in terms of this unity of God and
man. It will not be achieved, he says, far from it, by
explanation and abstraction, but by the quality of
personal life and personal dealing. The very fact that the
problems are more complex and the tensions sometimes
more unbearable than Froebel seems to have known
drives us back on the need for a faith which is ultimately
as simple and unified as was his.

Just as some have thought that Froebel's chief error in
his educational thinking was the assumption that knowledge or experience can be obtained from mere evolution
from within by making the inner, outer, so it is possible to
think that his mistake in religious thinking was similar.
The belief that man could evolve into godlikeness out of
his own self-activating will has always been inadequate,
and never more so than now. Just as in mental life the
eternal is formulated by the example and modified by it,
so any inner growth of persons happens in response to
something which comes to them from outside themselves.

This may come immediately by a response to other persons or communities, but ultimately it must come from some ultimate fact to which those persons are themselves responding. This fact for some is the Christian revelation "to wit that God was in Christ reconciling the world to Himself". If it is not that, it must be at least such a reality as gives unity to the whole of human experience and offers a faith by which to live. This, which is external to children, has to become their own as it interprets stage by stage their growing awareness of life. It is because Froebel maintained with great sincerity and repeated force that this essential religious function of education was its true nature, that he is speaking to our condition.

There has, indeed, been a response to Froebel in this country and America, as well as in his own, primarily because of his clear religious emphasis. Some have found that they could accept an educational theory which saw the goal in terms of unity with God; others have been able to see the religious significance of a system which so surely acknowledged the child as central. These are reasons which still weigh with some parents in sending their children to Froebel schools and their young people to Froebel training colleges. Froebel has at least a definite answer to the question this generation is so persistently asking: "Education for what?" He knew the value of a coherent pattern of educational thought and the unifying power of a religious impulse. In an age which has increasingly recognised the danger of educational specialisation, Froebel's principle of unity has taken on a contemporary importance; and in a time of secular thinking, some have found his Christian spirit an attractive approach. If today we find we accept neither his educational theory nor his Christian theology as adequate, we can still more readily and gratefully admit that he has indicated to us the task for our own time in his attempt to solve the problem of his own.

CHAPTER VI

FROEBEL'S EDUCATIONAL PHILOSOPHY IN 1952

1

EDUCATIONAL PHILOSOPHIES AND ULTIMATE PHILOSOPHIES: A GENERAL PROBLEM

I

THIS concluding chapter might be described as an attempt to reassess, in the broadest way, Froebel's educational outlook and teachings in the light of 1952. That would clearly mean, first of all, in the light of our actual growth in knowledge and understanding during the hundred years since his death. But on the very threshold of such an attempt there is a stumbling-block which can be—and most often is—disregarded, but which I think we do better to face.

It applies with particular force to Froebel, but is not by any means limited to his case. We cannot assess, or reassess, *any* educational philosophy as if it were simply a question of fact (or "the facts"). It is not like a scientific theory, or a technological advance, or even a scheme of practical reform in a field such as, let us say, that of public health. The light of 1952, as against 1852, is not all that is involved. To appreciate what *is* involved we have, I believe, only to glance at the problem as the case of Froebel presents it.

II

Earlier chapters have already shown how his great central principles of education have retained their vitality, but many of the applications which he himself most stressed have in our own day been discarded. It is not too difficult to give good reasons for this, which will be set out later; yet they leave a very perplexing question on our hands. Froebel's practical techniques, just as much as his main educational principles, flowed for him directly and necessarily from his total vision of the world. He was not of course a systematic philosopher, nor was he greatly interested in arguing or justifying his views; but he had his own comprehensive vision of the nature and foundation of the world and of man, which he held with fervent conviction. And for him the meaning and value of *every* part of his educational doctrines lay in that central faith; from this they all sprang, and this they were to provide with its living realisation and fulfilment.

What, then, happens if we reject what he saw as an integral part of an indivisible whole? Are we saying that the whole was *not* indivisible and that he just went astray in some part of his vision? Or are we, or some of us, perhaps not accepting this whole as such, but affirming the same central educational principles—let us say, education by the child's own activities and integrative growth—on quite different grounds? Are we possibly in the last analysis assessing his educational philosophy, and even his ultimate vision, by a divergent one of our own? And perhaps one of which he would not accept the very criteria, so that our judgment has little or no validity against him—or, indeed, for anyone who does not happen to agree with us beforehand?

We are not of course obliged to raise these questions—to say nothing of trying to answer them; and on the principle of leaving more or less well alone, we might be prudent in not doing so. But we can hardly render real justice to Froebel unless we face this challenge, and at the least try to define where, in seeking to reappraise his educational philosophy, we ourselves stand—and why.

III

The first need, in these circumstances, is to endeavour to see Froebel's own view in the round, as it appeared to him, and with the precise meaning and value which it had for him. I shall essay in fact, as far as a brief summary will allow, to trace out the way in which his basic world-vision led directly both to his central educational principles and to the concrete techniques that were to translate them into practice. It will then be possible to note, in proper perspective, some of the main impacts on his educational scheme of modern advances in factual knowledge and understanding both of the child and of our world at large. But that will only lead us back to the ultimate problem which, I believe, confronts everyone who really seeks to think out the fundamentals of where he stands in education. I do not think this problem, created by our clashing world views, is completely soluble but it seems to me no small part of Froebel's merit that, quite apart from his own world-vision, he has vitally contributed to the only working solution within our reach. This will be the burden of the concluding section of the present chapter; but before I make my attempt to recapture Froebel's own personal vision, it may be useful to try to state in a more general form the wider problem which lurks behind every serious educational discussion.

IV

I have spoken so far in terms of Froebel's particular case, but it is all too easy to enlarge the area of the dilemma. In the assessment of *any* educational philosophy, we are in the end involved in the issues of our own ultimate beliefs. Conversely, whatever creed we hold (even if it calls itself "none"), it can scarcely avoid having its own characteristic educational consequences and demanding its own educational philosophy. In the sphere of human education or upbringing there just is no room for a vacuum. The choice lies only between more or less blind or more or less fully-thought-out ways of filling it, or else letting it get filled. The moment we attempt to think out these ways we begin to get involved in selections and rejections, and therefore scales of values, and in the end problems of first or absolute preferences and the final good. Moreover, we must, or should, soon realise that if our thinking out is either only fractional or else too superficial, what is left unthought-out may swamp or defeat whatever outcome we do seek to plan. And again, utopian planning is one thing, practical prospects of achievement are another; for the latter purpose aims and methods must be shaped into the right relations to one another, and these must first be thought out or found out. In addition, plans may show only a semblance of achievement, without true reality, or may attain many different degrees or levels of reality. The further we carry our thinking out, the wider and more fundamental our *problem* becomes. We can readily see, indeed, that if we have an ultimate philosophy, and if it means anything, the educational sphere is the most important one in which its meaning must be fulfilled. But, conversely, once we begin to try to plan the plenum which the sphere of education *must* eventually become, we cannot *logically* (though we can all too well in practice) stop short of a complete and organic plan. And this is then simply the counterpart, in our world of action, of the implied theoretical philosophy of values on which we are willing to take our final stand.

This of course is no regression to a *tabula rasa* point of view, nor to that notion of the child as "a piece of wax or a lump of clay" against which Froebel so strongly inveighed. It is merely based on the inescapable facts of human infancy and childhood, and the inevitable growth of the human child into some form of membership of a human society. It would lose its main force only for infants brought up by wolves or goats, and even so only if they managed to keep away from human society until they had become entirely unhumanisable. From his first completely helpless and dependent stage up to the age of 12 to 20 years (according to the level of the surrounding civilisation), the child is so plastic to the community around him that whatever it does to him and whatever his own heritage, he cannot but assume its main outward likeness. In most cases, moreover, that likeness will not be outward only, but will penetrate some way into his character and personality, his dominant feelings and modes of action. And even if he finally turns away from his community or becomes a rebel against it, the very nature of his rebellion will be shaped by it and remain correlative to it. In the end the rebel and his rebellion will still "belong" as one element, together with all the others, within a larger social whole bearing the impress of a particular cultural pattern; and this in turn will have its own typical framework of unaware assumptions and untranscended horizons which will stamp it firmly as a society of a given period in time.

These facts, I think, must qualify any theory of educational freedom such as Froebel's as surely as any doctrine of deliberate moulding of the child. The differences between the two kinds of view remain of course fundamental, and will be returned to in our last section. For the moment what concerns us is only what is common to them both. Every theory of education must in the end be one of planned shaping, whether through "freedom" or through the opposite extreme of deliberate training and drilling, "teaching" and discipline. It can represent only such best conception as the educator feels able to form of the type of human individuals and human society he considers most worth while. And then his translation of this into such a scheme of selections and rejections, of influences and stimuli (planned over the whole plastic period of the child), as will build up the strongest prospect of his goal being attained. If with Froebel the freest possible members of the freest possible society are his aim, the ideal of freedom will no doubt permeate and shape every part of the educational plan. But all this is once more just one's ultimate choice of philosophy expressed in the most decisive field of planning and action that is open to human beings. Whether one has worked over an existing creed, or tried to formulate one's own independent philosophy, or has never thought out one's ultimate theoretical beliefs at all, the scale of preferences and values which one actually adopts in this most pregnant realm of human influence and power cannot be other than what one most believes.

If illustrations are desired, we need not go far to find them. The indissociable connection between ultimate creeds and theories of education meets us on every side. Any strongly held religious belief, whether Catholic or Protestant or Jewish or Mohammedan or Shinto, will as a matter of course seek to express itself in the process of education, and to transmit and if possible enhance itself through this. The same applies with scarcely less force to secular philosophies like those of rationalism or Marxism. And even if we turn to those educational reformers who expressly chose freedom for their watchword, we get each time a typical plan for this which springs directly from the basic philosophy of each thinker, whether he be Rousseau or Froebel, Herbert Spencer or John Dewey. In the case of those of us who have not carried our educational thinking through to completeness nor taken over an existing educational creed, the only reason why we are not committed to any single philosophy may well be that we have achieved none. We may be trying to make life easy for ourselves by a well-meaning but vague eclecticism which rests, in

Gift II

Gifts V and VI

fact, on a mere patchwork of unrelated or even contradictory basic values and beliefs.

V

Where all this finally leads to belongs to our later discussion. What is relevant here is its bearing on our
attempts to assess or reassess any given educational
philosophy. The dilemma is that, more or less inevitably,
we already have our own. This may be similar or different in *any* degree, from virtual identity to radical opposition and virtual incommensurability. Whatever it is, it
will of necessity enter into our assessment which will thus
unavoidably become question-begging. We shall in the
last resort approve and applaud what fits into our own
scheme and reject what does not. This of course is not the
whole story; even between the most disparate-seeming
philosophies there is usually some common ground on
which criticisms and comments are accepted as objective
by both. But just in the sphere of educational philosophy
it is peculiarly difficult either to define the boundary line
or to avoid passing beyond it. In practice we tend to have
something like an understanding, mostly tacit but sometimes explicit, that discussions shall not be pressed beyond
the point at which fundamental divisions of ultimate
belief come into view. The only alternative to this would
be to let every discussion of basic educational principles
become one of ultimate philosophies. In that case, however, any hope of agreement within the educational
field must be indefinitely postponed.

To bring this preliminary diagnosis round again to
Froebel's own case, we need, I think, refer back only to
the preceding chapter in the present volume. Mr.
Hamilton's discussion brings out in the most instructive
way, by practical demonstration, how inevitably basic
philosophy and educational philosophy are bound up

with one another. His assessing philosophy shares the same fundamental allegiance with the assessed one, but yet differs enough to make crystal clear how the whole plan and process of education must *respond* to the nature of the underlying ultimate beliefs. We are shown illuminatingly how even within the same creed, and indeed within the same broadest form of this, a difference of interpretation, as soon as it is fully worked out, carries its influence and its own informing spirit right through the ensuing educational philosophy. Mr. Hamilton's sympathetic, yet critical and searching study of Froebel's basic religious beliefs leads him to conclude that the latter has left out of account an essential element, perhaps indeed the most central one, of Christian truth—and also, by the same token, most of the great tract of universal human experience on which it rests. I cannot venture upon this issue, but, as it happens, from another angle, part of what follows in the present chapter gives its own support to Mr. Hamilton's critique. In fact, the philosophy of education to which it leads seems to me to supply an essential corrective to Froebel even from my rather different point of view. Nevertheless, for Mr. Hamilton the link with a particular Christian theology and what this means for him not only remains, but is all-important. On the other side, full Froebelians of our own day might still wish both to maintain the master's religious philosophy and to insist in their turn that it *is* truly Christian. There might perhaps also be others, not necessarily Froebelians, who would regard their philosophy as Christian in essence, but would want to range themselves more nearly with Froebel's than with Mr. Hamilton's point of view. In any such cases, the debate would necessarily have to move over to the theological field; and the derivativeness and dependence of any "merely" educational philosophy as such would once more be made manifest.

2

FROEBEL'S DOCTRINE AS A UNITARY WHOLE

VI

There I must leave the dilemma for the time being and turn to Froebel's philosophy, basic and educational, in the meaning it bore for him.

Let me begin by recalling very briefly the main heads of Froebel's vision of God and nature and man; I need not do more, since Mr. Hamilton has presented so adequate a picture of his religious philosophy as a whole. My object will, in fact, only be to bring into focus those primary ideas which carried him on directly, first to his main educational principles and then—as he felt, with the same force—to the techniques and practices which for a while seemed his most personal contribution to early education. What I chiefly wish to set in relief here, for the reasons already stated, is the continuity and singleness of his total view.

In the broadest philosophic perspective: the universe is the living work and manifestation of God. Everything flows from Him and expresses Him and testifies to Him. Nature and man alike embody the principle of divinity as their very being and essence, and exist solely in order to bring this to fulfilment. But man, and man alone, can achieve direct consciousness and knowledge of his divinity, direct consciousness of his destiny, and so, by free self-determination, the attainment of this destiny and the direct sense of unity with God. Man grows into that consciousness and knowledge in so far as he fully realises his own growth. And he accomplishes this in so far as, through his own activity, he freely develops every side of his nature, through every progressive stage according to its own inherent law, in harmonious unison. But every human being is born as a member of a family and a community and a nation, and he can achieve his own growth only as a harmonious part of these larger wholes. And they in turn represent different realms of unity through which mankind realises by progressive stages its total growth towards the divine. Different eras of mankind have their different tasks or their different parts of the same task; each successive era can and must achieve higher levels of consciousness of the divine and of approach to unity with God. The goal of all human history, individual and collective, is unification; first, the unification of each individual's whole life within himself; then the unification of his life with that of nature and his fellow-men; and finally his unification with God.

Given the nature of man as a conscious being with an inner as well as an outer life, the activities whereby he achieves his growth will of necessity be of two main kinds, which must continually go on side by side. On the one hand, starting from within himself, he must constantly seek to embody in outward form the principle of divinity and unity which is striving for expression in him; and so in endlessly different ways he is impelled to depict, to fashion and *create*. On the other hand, he must constantly strive to take into himself the picture of the world he finds outside him; to discover in it all the forms and laws by which it manifests its unity; in a word, to seek out the divine, wherever he can reach it, by the way of *knowledge*. Each person is a unique individual who has the power and the vocation to express the divine principle within him by his own creative activities in his own distinctive mode. But each person also needs to find for himself the universal laws, and the universal unity and divinity, in the plurality and diversity and manifoldness of the world outside him.

Progress in knowledge proceeds by the universal laws of opposition and mediation, whereby to each thing or quality or happening there is an opposite within the

same kind, through which it can be most fully apprehended and defined; and then for each such pair of
opposites there must be sought, and can be found, an
intermediate term whereby they can be reconciled and
unified. Thus the principle of unity in diversity and
manifoldness is continually re-achieved and enlarged.
And by this advance (through opposition and mediation)
from synthesis to synthesis, wider and higher levels of
unification are continually attained.

The divine principle in each human being is the direct
root of religion. He needs and strives from the start to
grow towards God; that is the final meaning of all his
growth, but finds its clearest expression in the unfolding
of his conscious, explicit religious feeling and awareness
of God. In effect, at the end all his progress in knowledge
and insight, action and creation, is growth into religion
and in religion, and growth towards and into that holy
life which signifies communion and union with God.

VII

This schematic summary cannot do justice to Froebel's
own endless variations on all the above themes, his
mystical elaborations of them, his impassioned belief in
them and apostolic proclamation of them. Much, moreover, is left out; in particular the ways in which he links
his general deistic (or even near-pantheistic) principles
with his fervent Christian creed—his stress on the principle of triuneness in God and nature and man, the meaning he assigns in his world to the person of Jesus Christ,
and all his insistence on the vital place in education of
Christian teachers and Christian teaching. With these
aspects of Froebel's world view, Mr. Hamilton has already
fully dealt. I have tried to re-state here only that central
core of beliefs which leads almost self-evidently to his distinctive educational doctrines. What now are the doc-

trines to which such a vision of the world and man must lead?

Again, I can only summarise:

(i) The whole purpose of education must of necessity be to foster the realisation of the divine principle in man.

(ii) This principle is not something to be implanted or inculcated or "taught". It is there, in every child, by virtue of the origin and nature of man and of the whole universe. It has only to be left free to create its own fulfilment. Thus any plan or process of education that seeks to achieve its aim by inculcation from without is fundamentally wrong. In fact, any education that does not base itself throughout on the child's own inward growth must be wrong. Any conception of education which treats him as if he were "a piece of wax or a lump of clay" to be moulded by the educator is a crime against the very nature—and the divinity—of the child.

(iii) Where this basic error or this crime is committed the effect cannot but be disastrous. It cannot impose any different nature on the child, but it can prevent his true nature from being realised. It can choke or starve, arrest or pervert, his own inward growth. Wrong beliefs about the child and wrong treatment based on this, or even the mere lack of true understanding of him, must inevitably lead either to active interference with his growth or, at best, to grave failure to foster it. The true theory of education must start by acknowledging both his real nature and the true laws of his development, and must aim throughout at respecting these. Just as it is possible, either by wrong beliefs or by default, to impose on the child conditions which will stunt or hamper this development, so by right understanding we can provide those conditions which will do most to promote it. The one guiding criterion must of course be actual growth. And, what is more, harmonious growth in every direction and in optimal degree.

(iv) It follows that the educator who acknowledges the divine principle in the child seeking to realise itself through his growth must first of all strive to learn all the laws and processes of this growth. Only so can he know both the general setting which it needs all the time, and the specific needs of each of its particular forms and stages. Thus he must study every factor that counts in the course of children's development, both generically and individually. And not only must he bring to bear in the shaping of their educational conditions all that he has grasped so far, but he must always be ready to learn afresh in each unique individual case.

(v) It follows equally that the first condition of all education is the utmost freedom for the child. Since he has in him his own living principle of growth, and if left free must grow in the way that matters most, it is his foremost right to be thus left free to grow. But that must mean freedom to act and move, and unfold on every side, since it is by these means alone that he can realise his growth. Such freedom is indeed a very condition for the educator's task; only from the child who is given full scope to develop in his own way, without any constraint or deforming force applied from without, can he hope to learn the detailed processes and laws of his growth.

(vi) It follows next that in order to realise the divine principle within himself, the child, in the measure in which he is left free, will continually and actively *seek growth*. He will do so by the successive deployment and exercise and enjoyment of his every power, in the great growth-enacting and growth-promoting cycle of activities which we call his *play*. Through this all that is latent in him finds expression and secures development. Each of his powers in turn is carried forward through being freely exercised, and plays its part in a single, comprehensive and harmonious movement of advance. Play is the fundamental medium and instrument through which the child, out of his own impulses and inward resources, effects his own growth in every direction that is open to him. The educator has only to learn how to provide the widest opportunities and means, as well as the fullest freedom, for such play. The criterion of his success will then clearly be the child's own zest and delight, which he draws from every achievement and which then leads him on joyously to new achievement and advance.

(vii) Applying his principle that we must first follow the process of growth so that we may then foster it, Froebel finds in this process just those modes of striving for the divine which his world-vision had already led him to expect. The two great ways of growth which, as we have seen, ensue from the complementary inner and outer life of man can be watched in action almost from the start. They certainly become apparent soon after the child achieves his first mastery of limbs and speech and the handling of objects in the outer world. The more he is left free, the more surely we shall find him trying all the time to make the outer inner, to draw it within himself, to turn it into his own lasting possession. If he is given the least chance, we can observe him continually and eagerly looking and listening and touching, manipulating and experimenting, exploring and discovering. And in the same way he may be constantly seen, with no less eagerness, striving to make the inner outer, expressing and enacting, depicting and fashioning, constructing and inventing. We may note how he does so by every sort of dramatic make-believe and play, by drawing and painting, by moulding in clay, by building with bricks and sand and everything he can lay hold of, in fact by using as a medium anything that will enable him to body forth his imaginings and to create things out of his own mind and by his own hands. Those are the ways in which, left free, he grows, and by his own activities forms and educates himself.

In these processes Froebel claims that the educator (now turned child-psychologist) will readily discern the typical continuous seeking for *unity*, which the divine principle in the child demands. He will note a typical restlessness till it is found, a half-way pre-divination of its nature, and an eager and gratified welcoming of it when found. In the process of learning, the effort is to combine, integrate and understand; comparisons are constantly applied; what is discovered is marshalled and arranged; connecting questions are asked, links and relations are sought, natural symmetries or unified forms are eagerly responded to and hailed with delight. In the process of expressing and designing and making, the child visibly tries to create unity, to fashion balanced forms and patterns, to invent or discover rhythms, and to build integral wholes. His powers for a long time fall far short of his needs and strivings; but how he welcomes rhymes and tunes, patterns and pictures, wholes or unities which he sees taking shape in front of him; and with what zest, as soon as he can make the first gestures towards this, he is ready to join! The educator's part once more is only to furnish the opportunities and encouragement whereupon the child will freely deploy his own activities and provide his own exploration and learning, enjoyment and creation.

(viii) Furthermore, Froebel holds that he can show from the beginning the child's need for a sense of communion and oneness with those around him. He is a member of a family and seeks the feeling of family unison—unison with his mother, with his father, with his brothers and sisters. He is brought together with other children, and again he soon wants to enter into an active relation of joint and harmonious play with them; and so with other adults and the larger groups of the school and the community. Always the same striving for unity in diversity, for concord and solidarity; the need to grow into a family and a community and a society, and at length the society of mankind, as a member of the whole participating in its life and contributing his own share to it. The educator's task, in this as in every other field, is only to provide the means; to ensure that the child will not lack access to harmonious groups of playmates, and later on larger and more enduring communities of fellow-learners, fellow-players and fellow-workers, into which he can grow.

(ix) Finally this last aspect of the process of growth brings us most directly to one of the most revolutionary changes in earlier attitudes to education which the Froebelian philosophy of human unfolding demands. Since the child's development is a continuous and cumulative story from the start, it is clear that what is most vital of all is that its *beginnings* should be right. It is they that must be most carefully shielded from everything that could distort or impede them, and most understandingly provided with those conditions which can best aid and foster them. For in them lies the root of everything that follows; anything wrong with them must project its warping or limiting influence through the whole rest of the child's growth, with accumulating effect.

Froebel holds in fact, consistently with his fundamental beliefs, that if a child shows any evil traits or serious defects of character and behaviour, there can be no other explanation for these (since they cannot spring from his own nature) than grave faults of handling in his first all-important years.

Thus the most significant period for education is just that of infancy and the pre-school age which conventional educational doctrines had so commonly neglected; and the phase of the very greatest moment is that earliest one when the infant is still wholly or mainly under his mother's care, so that it is she who is the most important of educators.

It follows therefore that those concerned with the education of educators and forced to think out the theory of human upbringing as a whole must, as one of their chief tasks, impress on the world the vital part played by these earliest years. And they must insist on the need to ensure that rightly trained helpers should dedicate themselves to these years—and, above all, that mothers should understand their great privilege and power, and accept in all its consequences their natural dedication to this supreme task.

VIII

The foregoing may perhaps suffice to show how starting from basic first principles we are carried, via broad educational theory and perspective, directly into the realm of typical Froebelian practice. This developed throughout as the immediate logical outcome of his theory.

There was first of all the great concept of the kindergarten (though, as we know, this name for it was not found for some time). Young children were to be regarded and tended essentially like plants. Like these, if they were given the right conditions, they would grow and unfold and flower, by their own law, each according to its individual capacity and destiny. The educator, like a good gardener, had only to provide them with the right conditions. The kindergarten was the place where these were solicitously assembled, and where trained "child-gardeners" took over from the mother as the child became ready to seek a larger community than the home and to grow towards full membership of the wider human society for which he was destined.

But the kindergarten was itself only a further expansion and fulfilment of the meaning of the home. And it had to lead on in turn to the more formal and systematic school, guided and inspired by the same spirit. Therefore there was the invocation, first and foremost to mothers, but equally to kindergarten teachers, and then also to teachers generally and, indeed, in some sense to the community at large: "Come, let us live for our children." There, for Froebel, lay the greatest possibilities and hopes for the future—if only everyone could be led to understand what the child sought and needed. And of what he was capable if in the right spirit of dedication his seekings were shared, the ways of advance were opened before him and his needs were met.

And so there was Froebel's own attempt to think out all those needs and to work out the best ways of being *ready for them,* and thus turning them into opportunities for optimal growth. There was the series of his own practical contributions to what he held to be the ideal succession of earliest play-objects, the ideal materials for individual formative activities and the most educative forms of group play. There were the typical rhymes and pictures by which mothers could guide their infants to all the different kinds of experience and learning, the shared feelings and thoughts and understanding, they inwardly sought. There were the model ways by which mothers and teachers could help children to express progressively their own world of feeling and imagination in song and drawing. There were, in effect, all the characteristic Froebelian techniques, the gifts and occupations, the *Mutter und Koselieder,* the various stepwise procedures of "natural" teaching, the great variety of rhythmic and patterned group-games.

But all this was of course for Froebel totally different from any previous formal education by outward "teaching" or instruction. It rested for him directly on the principle of the child's own growth, which he was merely understanding beforehand and striving always to meet half-way. The child being what he is, it lies, as we have seen, in the very essence of his growth that he must continually seek and find unity in diversity, the primal forms and patterns of things, the laws that govern the universe, the progressive stepping-stones to the divine. The more he can be helped towards this in every field— but always in the end by his own experience and activity, both from without inward and from within outward— the freer and more abundant and more satisfying will be his growth.

Thus we get all the typical forms of Froebel's help to the child, drawn direct from the fountainhead of his ultimate vision and beliefs. The sphere is the primal form of forms, the most pregnant and significant, and indeed also the ultimate one. The ball must therefore be the understanding educator's first gift to the child. But in our world there are endless other forms, including such as must seem most antithetical to the sphere. The child's own great inward law of learning is by opposition and mediation. Therefore he will take the most welcoming delight in the contrast and difference of the second gift, the cube, the very symbol of diversity as such. His world is now at once immensely widened. Yet difference is always only the second, not the final word. Difference is essentially a stimulus and a problem. The first solution to this first problem, the key principle and archetype for an unending vista of such solutions in the most varied settings, is that mediating and reconciling intermediary form, the cylinder. These three gifts in their succession and their relation are symbolic of, and pregnant with, the whole future intellectual growth of the child.

Yet though he will get endless pleasure and fulfilment from his play with them, and through this will carry with him a potent beginning in insight which will help to guide him throughout his life, these objects can satisfy one side of his nature only, the grasping and understanding one. The *divided* cube links up with what went before, but opens up in its own distinctive right a quite different avenue of growth—growth through his own activities of combination and separation, arrangement and construction, and the realisation of fantasy in the very world of fact. And so with all the next stages and all the other specially devised occupations and forms of activity. Space does not permit any further detailed analysis here, but the principle throughout is that every time the child shall be provided in the simplest and most appropriate form with the very thing, the very stimulus, the next step, which the inward necessity of growth in him most needs and seeks.

So in their different way with the *Mutter und Koselieder*; they express the feelings which the child must want to hear expressed; the obscure divinations to which he wants names and outward forms given; the ways of learning for which he most gropes and longs. So with the organised social games, with their circles and patterns and complex rhythmic evolutions and recitations. So with all the little songs and rhymes accompanying various activities in which the children speak of themselves as joyous and happy and kind and good and this and that, because that is how they actually feel, and must feel. So with the later more formal instruction in arithmetic and geometry, speech forms and drawing, natural history and elementary science, in which the children are continually steered in the direction of those formal and logical relations which they must be seeking out of their own nature, and in which, when they uncover them, they must find so much satisfaction and delight.

IX

We must note, as we look back over our course, that Froebelian practical education, as he himself planned and shaped it, is not after all something as studiously passive and merely permissive as the first impact of his theory might have led us to conclude. We finish up with quite a formidable didactic scheme, with its own rules of proper application, even for very young children; a formidable degree of direction of the child's activities, through the continuous and pervasive operation of this scheme (of methods as well as objects and materials); and a formidable syllabus of later formal instruction pivoted on the assumption that the world of mathematical and logical relations is the intellectual goal which in the end every child wishes to reach, and can and should reach. It is all quite consistent (though obviously the attractive analogy of plants and gardeners, whilst it embodies one vital side of the truth, is not meant by Froebel himself to be pressed too far). This scheme of education never signifies for Froebel any imposition from without; it is only a set of optimal aids to fulfilment of the very aims pursued by the inward growth of the child himself. And we cannot but note how strongly Froebel insisted that each of his practical applications of his basic principles was fully supported by the great criterion, inherent within the child, which from the beginning he had laid down. He constantly repeated his claim that both the direct responses of the children in his various schools—that is, the touchstone of their actual zest and delight—and their thriving and enduring growth provided the living demonstration of the rightness of his way.

And yet we have the fact that progressive education-ists, at any rate in this country, have very largely turned away from most of the practical Froebelian scheme outlined above. The reasons for this are, I think, irresistible. It is not merely—as even full Froebelians would agree—that the gifts and occupations, etc., might all too easily lend themselves to mechanical use by the ill-trained, un-trained or unintelligent, in a way that might make them worse than useless for education. It is that the entire scheme rests to a great extent on insufficient or erroneous child psychology. Even that, indeed, is not all that is wrong, but the next section will deal more fully with this question. Meanwhile, however, we are left with the sustained success claimed both by Froebel himself and by his strict followers, together with the challenge this presents to those of us who accept his touchstone. At least a partial answer may well be that an enthusiastic and gifted teacher can carry with him children who come under his personal influence even by methods which lack general value or validity; and this would hold not only for Froebel himself, but equally for those with similar gifts in whom he or his doctrine had kindled the same enthusiasm. A further factor might, I fear, be the fatal ease with which any scheme of education, in skilled hands, can secure an appearance of response and successful results of the kind it aims at through the mere social plasticity of most children. Froebelian technique would then simply be no worse, but no better, than any other outwardly imposed (though not inwardly true) scheme of education. But a full answer must, I think, also include the fact that there is so much that *is* true and significant in Froebel's child psychology that even those elements in his technique which we believe we must now reject are still capable of producing results of some value. The minimal form of our criticism would then be that they produce limitations as well as positive results; that these results are not now those which we most want to attain; and that certainly Froebel's scheme, taken as a whole, no longer represents the most fruitful approach open to us. It is not practicable here to assess more closely what part these various possible components might play in a complete answer. The problem remains one that merits pondering, but it cannot affect the general criticisms of Froebel's educational philosophy and child psychology which the sheer advance of our knowledge and understanding since his time has brought with it.

The next section will seek to indicate some of the main impacts of this advance—particularly in child psychology, but also to some extent in our general picture of our world—on the factual assumptions and beliefs upon which Froebel's educational philosophy rested. That, however, will bring us back only to our original fundamental problem, to which the last section of this chapter will again address itself.

3

The Impact of Latter-day Knowledge, above all Psychological

X

If we turn now first of all to Froebel's actual picture of the child, I think we must say, in the light of our more modern knowledge, that it is far too simple on the one hand and far too idealised on the other. This of course does not lessen our great debt to him as a pioneer among those who insisted on direct study of the child, throughout all the processes and stages and forces of his growth, as a first prerequisite for any plan for "educating" him. But the gathering momentum of the process he himself thus helped to launch has swept away much of the ground on which he thought he could most firmly take his stand; and in particular the last half-century of intensive study of the child has altered the picture of him as Froebel envisaged it in at least the following major ways:

1. The great body of work on the comparative measurement of intelligence has established, at least broadly, that every child is born with a definite endowment of general ability (whether high or average or low) which education can usually do little to change. There is a controversial margin to this work, and some evidence

precisely that "free" and understanding educational methods can produce a limited rise of level in many or even most children, and perhaps a considerable rise in a few. But we are only too safe in dismissing from our hopes today any idea that by suitably varying our educational techniques we could turn a group of children with I.Q.s of 95–105 into the same group with I.Q.s of 145–155. For we are not dealing here with a merely conventional or statistical index without intrinsic importance. There is an irresistible weight of evidence that our comprehensive batteries of intelligence tests measure, even if imperfectly, something all too real. The difference between an I.Q. of 100 and one of 150 is something innate and radical, which confronts the educator in every field, and in the last resort gives the measure of an individual's very capacity for intellectual growth. The more we believe in education, not by parrot-teaching or cramming or drilling but by real inward understanding and integrative growth, the more we must accept the inherent limits set by widely different innate *capacities for growth*. Logical relations or real situations or intellectual problems above a certain level of complexity appear to be right outside the grasp of that large mass of the population which under our current tests registers an I.Q. of 100 or less; and we have no grounds for believing that either the earliest start or the most understanding methods or the finest gradations in presentation can change that state of affairs. Ever since teaching first began, eager teachers have been driven to despair by this fact, or, still worse, to exasperated but futile attempts to achieve their object somehow by sheer main force; but now at least they can be resigned and tolerant about it, because it is not their fault, and not even that of their charges.

Of course no one can set any bounds to such revolutionary *new* discoveries in psychology (or perhaps physiology) as the future may bring; but according to our best present knowledge we just cannot legislate educationally—at least in the intellectual field—for the child as such. We must think in terms of a hierarchy of levels of capacity and reach, and accept the inborn limitations of the lower levels. That, indeed, does not lessen the value of an educational approach wholly directed to and guided by the true integrative growth of every child. On the contrary, it only makes this all the more vital. And we must redouble our efforts to find ways by which, as far as ever possible, we can bring within the scope even of those with more limited capacities every main aspect of our human heritage. Our power of doing this, however, depends precisely on our *understanding* of the maximum rate at which they can advance and the final limits of what they can attain.

2. There is equally all the allied work on the measurement of special abilities. Here again something which had in the past been widely but loosely assumed, but which Froebel from his *a priori* standpoint had largely brushed aside, has now been established as a plain, indubitable fact. Froebel, whilst he certainly insisted on the element of unique individuality in each child, was most concerned with the nature and needs of his universal humanity. He took little or no cognisance of any intermediate groupings; in the last resort what he contemplated was the Platonic reality "Man", of which each individual child alike was an instance, with the same divine principle in each seeking fulfilment in *essentially* the same ways. Every child had his own personality and gifts, but at the same time, in virtue of the divinity within him, must be equally capable of everything "universally" human. But we now know that besides their widely differing levels of general intelligence or innate capacity for intellectual growth, children fall into various classes or groups marked by very diverse special abilities; by the lack or near lack of some, and by high

or low degrees of others. And, unfortunately for Froebel's standpoint, among the most unequally distributed of these "special abilities" are just those which he thought the most universal and vital vehicles of *all* human growth: drawing, music and mathematics. These are facts which we must accept as we find them: our educational approach must acknowledge the great natural differences among children in these and other "special abilities", and indeed must base itself on them. We can try our utmost, on general human grounds, to make good some deficiencies of this type, as far as ever the response of the children will allow; but in the main we must strive to find, within their range, their own positive capacities for fruitful activity and growth.

3. There have been the monumental investigations, over the last thirty years, of Professor Piaget and his collaborators, on every aspect of mental development: language and modes of thought, logical judgment and reasoning, picture of the world and notion of causality, sense of time, space and reality, number and geometrical forms, moral ideas and moral judgment, etc. A good deal in Professor Piaget's interpretations of his results has aroused discussion and doubt, and it has been suggested that his work presents only one side of the picture, which needs to be completed by a different and more dynamic approach. But even if this is true, his side of the picture is there, and presents a vast and comprehensive canvas of *average* mental development which cannot in future be left out of account. In the general evolution of his ideas each child advances (whether more slowly or more quickly, according to his native intelligence and opportunities), through a long series of distinguishable stages from an initial phase of mainly ego-centric, syncretistic, fantasy-governed thinking, to the very gradual conquest of reciprocal, relational and objectively controlled thought. Even so he only achieves this at first in concrete

situations; a further prolonged evolution is required till he attains that level also (at least in some degree) in abstract logical form. The first stage of this conquest is generally achieved only by *average* children at 7–8 years, and the second as late as 10–12 years. The great array of Professor Piaget's experimental studies in field after field is so impressive, so consistent and so powerfully inter-supporting that no one today can doubt the substantial correctness and revealingness of his work. No attempt can be made here to do justice to this, and no discussion is possible of its relation to the equally strong evidence for the complementary approach. Only passing reference can be made to its basis in the free-ranging, eager, penetrating logic and judgment which we can watch at work in every lively, intelligent child from as early as his third or fourth year onwards, in situations of *spontaneous* interest and inquiry. Thus Piaget's work must not in any circumstances be allowed to exclude methods of education which encourage and promote these situations and expressly seek to pick up all the growing points, the numerous moments of vision and truth, in every child. Indeed, as is well known, he has himself been linked for many years with the practice of "free" educational techniques at the Maison des Petits in Geneva. Nevertheless, his results stand as a measure of the range and magnitude and length of the task of *all-round* maturation and integration which every child must work through; a measure which leaves no room for the easy simplicity of the Froebelian view.

4. There is a further large and ever-growing body of psychological work of which we must at least take cognisance, although it has hardly as yet passed beyond the exploratory and tentative level. It carries us over from the intellectual field into the no less crucial one of personality and character, and covers all modern inquiries both into individual traits with their variations,

and also into possible groupings by dominant traits or trait-constellations and "types". The impediments to progress in this field are many and deep-reaching; the assumptions behind much of the work hitherto done are somewhat dubious, and the right approach to fruitful experimental work (if there is one) may still be undiscovered. Nevertheless, we are now aware, at the least, how much there is still to be learnt in this realm. We cannot shut our minds to the high probability of individual wide differences of *inborn* disposition or temperament, and to the possibility also of varying native personality-*types* or character-*types*. Eventually we may learn how we can most pregnantly distinguish and grade the former, and perhaps also how (if they exist) we can segregate out the latter and use them as keys for stable and enduring groupings. We cannot of course predict the rate of this progress or define in advance what may prove to be its limits; the one thing that is certain, however, is the vital relevance of what we can or cannot achieve here to the process of education. If the latter is to seek its ends within the child and base itself on his own potentialities and inward development, it must begin by acknowledging the extraordinary difficulties of the field of human personality and temperament, as the very disappointments and failures of so much of our psychological work have impressed them on us. And whilst our theory of education seeks to learn all it can, even if only negatively, from what has already been done or tried, it must keep in continuous and even anxious touch with all further work that shows any promise of progress. Froebel's own outlook inevitably belongs to an age before the very nature (to say nothing of the complexity) of these problems had risen above the horizon.

5. The foregoing refers only to the great mass of specific researches into personality, temperament and character problems carried out by modern so-called

"academic" psychologists; that is, by workers operating or at least trained in psychological laboratories and universities. But whilst this work has so far brought little in the way of conclusive results, we can hardly now avoid accepting the deep change in our *general* picture of the child and his inward life and history which we owe first of all to the development of psycho-analysis. Here again there is much which is still regarded by many people as controversial. Thanks, however, to the very stimulus of psycho-analysis, there has ensued a large body of direct behaviouristic observation and study of young children, which has already amply confirmed many of the most striking features in the new analytic picture of the child. Indeed, when once, with the help of psycho-analysis, we have discarded our traditional blinkers, we can only too easily see for ourselves how much has had to be newly discovered which we might long since have foreseen. Any *adequate* genetic psychology, genuinely focused on the child, on the whole child and nothing but the child, and seeking without preconceptions to trace through his story from what we all know and can observe of him, ought to have led to very much the same dramatic outline as psycho-analysis has revealed to us.

In order to minimise controversial issues, I propose here only to glance briefly at that outline in so far as (whatever its *historical* debt) it does not need to depend on psycho-analysis. That is, in so far as it can be drawn from general psychological knowledge and insight, and can in the main be directly supported by observable facts. The point of central importance seems to me to be the inevitable and vivid *drama*, the tensions and crises and conflicts, which must be at the core of the experience of every child from his first few months onward. At that time his feeling-life is already capable of the utmost intensity (there is behaviouristic evidence how early he can *manifest* fear and rage, and we have every reasonable ground for holding that as he behaves so he *feels*); but the life of knowledge and action has scarcely begun. Thus during that first phase the drama of his feeling-life not only occupies the centre of the stage, but has this virtually to itself. Feeling therefore cannot but be extreme and absolute; nothing that could moderate or balance or diffuse it is there yet. The moderating factors only come in slowly, and their powers remain very limited until something like middle childhood; moreover, they are partly counteracted, even as they begin to take shape, by the concurrent development of fantasy, which all too readily operates to add new fuel and strength to the overriding sway of feeling. This would appear to be particularly true of the fantasies that express and sustain fear and rage and jealousy and frustrated desire; those that serve our more pleasant states, though often equally vivid and strong, are apt to show far less power of maintaining themselves against the advancing tide of knowledge and fact (and we cannot even regret this).

The actual condition of the infant throughout at least his first year is one of complete helplessness and dependence. And nothing that can be done in any normal environment can save him from being frequently and intensely made to *feel* this state. As we know all too well, his absolute desires cannot all on the instant be fulfilled, nor can their fulfilment, when it comes, always go on as long as he wants it to. He must sometimes suffer not being immediately satisfied, or even not being succoured at once in distress; he must suffer on occasions being refused or restrained or stopped; he must not infrequently suffer finding himself alone and not being successful in summoning the saving presence forthwith, or, still worse, being actually left by her against all his struggles and protests. All these are for him at first absolute and boundless hurts or ills; he is utterly helpless to do anything about them, and can only react in the one way within his power, which is to rage and cry, to fear and despair. And these things befall him from the very person on whom he most depends, with whom his life is most bound up, to whom he looks for all his satisfactions and happiness and help. So that he cannot avoid being drawn into conflicting feelings about her; the greater the love and joy with which he stretches out to her and communes with her, the more open he lies also to the bewildering, the incomprehensible frustrations and denials and desertions which at other times seem to him to come from her; and to the rages and fears with which on these occasions he cannot help responding to them and to her. The positive, loving states will of course mostly predominate in any happy child-mother relationship; but only conventional blindness, or our time-honoured selective and distorting spectacles, can prevent us from realising that the other, negative and at least temporarily hostile passions must also be there. And they are hardly likely to be lessened (even though they may more and more be pressed into the background) when the infant first practises his new-found power of biting and is restrained and rebuffed; or when presently he goes through the first great crisis of weaning; or when he increasingly experiences the processes and pressures of "habit-training", etc., etc.

These patterns thereafter become less absolute as the wider world of perception and skill and action comes in. But by way of another chapter which cannot but go on, how can the child avoid feeling the tension of his rivalry with his father for his mother's attention and love, and with his mother for his father's attention and love (an unavoidable plain fact inherent in the situation, even if we resist its full psycho-analytic interpretation)? And how can he escape a major new crisis with the advent of a brother or sister who *must* largely or partly *displace* him in the attention and care and devotion of his mother?

How can he tell, out of his own resources, as he actually, day by day, suffers the displacement, that this is not the end, or the beginning of the end, of all things for him? And unless he is more than human, how in his heart of hearts can he respond with anything else but distress and fear and, above all, jealousy and hate? Wisdom and forethought and a redoubled loving-kindness, both before and after, can indeed do much to mitigate the crisis, especially in children beyond their first few years; but even so they cannot alter the underlying facts or prevent them from hurting and arousing new anxiety, and at the same time reviving *old* hurts and *old* anxieties, at any rate in some degree.

And in all these situations, of which at least some come to every child, what in the world can avail to save him from that fatal *inner* gift of fantasy—from the overpowering imaginings that intensify and prolong and endlessly renew in variegated forms the feelings to which he is a prey, and ring all the possible changes on anxieties that may already be too strong for him?

And so we get real children, and their real story which, even if often predominantly happy, is inherently incapable of being a pure and unalloyed idyll. We get most frequently a greater or less degree of all the familiar troubles and problems and distresses of childhood. We begin to understand that these are not necessarily just accidental or random. We may realise that there is more than meets the eye in sudden stubbornnesses or shynesses or social difficulties; in feeding fads or refusals or resistances to food; in night terrors and screaming fits and temper tantrums; in the onset, apparently out of the blue, of obsessive or compulsive fantasies or actions; in bed wetting or masturbation or all sorts of other aberrations of behaviour or sudden cessations of growth or even retrogressions from it. And we may see all the more clearly that these things must mean something which is not merely fortuitous but may

be very deep-rooted when we find that they happen even
with children who had appeared to adapt equably and
well to all the demands and conditions of their estate;
that they happen even to the children of psychologists
and psycho-analysts and others who (at least in earlier
days) thought they knew what was needed, did all that
required to be done, and avoided whatever had to be
avoided. Psycho-analysts, in particular, were at one time
disposed to think, under the influence of their first great
sense of understanding and insight, that now the way to
free and unimpeded and happy growth lay open for
every child. One had only to lift from him the traditional
artificial pressures and restraints and inhibitions, which
could be shown to split and warp him. Rather like
Froebel, they tended to see in early mistakes and mishandlings the sole root of all childish evil. But this belief
or hope could not survive the test. Over and over again
it appeared that even where every conceivable care had
been taken to avoid every known mistake, to keep everything negative or disturbing or potentially warping away
from a given child, sooner or later the same familiar
pattern of fear-fantasies and behaviour-difficulties made
itself manifest again.

Thus there was nothing for it in the end but to accept
the insight to which clinical work and theory had also
more and more led. No outward adjustment can avail
to save any child completely from the succession of inward crises which is inherent in the very nature both of
his own feeling-and-fantasy life and of his initial relation
with the world around him, but, above all, with those
who matter most to him in it. We may then believe, with
one school of thought, that an aggressive, destructive,
hating instinct is an original part of our human endowment as much as a loving and unifying and constructive
one. Or with another group, we may set up the interesting hypothesis of an innate, self-directed, regressive

death-instinct which the opposing and stronger life-instinct succeeds in deflecting from its original aim and turning outward, thus first converting it into a force of external hate and destructiveness. Or we may leave these questions open and merely note how from his first few months the infant is forced by his experiences of helplessness and distress and rage and fear into endless negative and self-conflicting states, which are thus woven into the first basic pattern of his life and then continually revived and strengthened by countless new situations of a comparable kind, with their new frustrations and crises. Whichever of these views we adopt, the one picture which I think we can no longer retain is that of the infant whose life is all happiness and goodness and content and who has only to be spared gratuitous mistakes or mishandlings to grow from bliss to bliss into untroubled and joyous and more and more nearly divine perfection. The Froebelian vision of the child is a dream. It does not, in fact, do justice to his grandeurs any more than to his miseries, as he goes through life struggling with the inward problem of his divisions and conflicts. He carries with him indeed, not far below the surface, first into his school community and then into adult social life, the same liability to fall back into helplessness and dependence; the same fear of frustration and defeat; the same anxiety and fear at large, and the same anger and hate and jealousy and rivalry; but also the same need and capacity for friendship and sympathy and love, the same stretching out for them, and the same running battle between these opposed forces, with their alternating bids for victory. That remains the perennial theme of human history; and it is not by denying it but, on the contrary, only by its full recognition and understanding that education can contribute its share—potentially perhaps the most decisive share—to aid the forces of construction and harmony to win.

XI

These, then, are some of the chief elements in our changed picture of the child. What now of our changed picture of the world?

On this I can touch only very lightly, again with the avoidance as far as is possible of what is controversial, and no room for more than a few selected indications of general trends.

1. Since Froebel's day there has been an immense expansion in our sheer factual knowledge of our world. Strictly empirical and inductive science has come to play a much larger part than before relatively to the deductive-mathematical disciplines. The logic of induction and scientific method has taken its full place side by side with the older deductive or formal logic, and, indeed, would be accepted by many modern students of thought as the fundamental logic of *learning*. Biology has acquired a new status and a new significance through the theory of evolution. Whole new empirical sciences and branches of science have been developed. We know vastly more about the limitless diversity and surprisingness of our world, in the remoter realms of space, in the sphere of microscopic life, in all the ways of living things, even in the complex empirical composition and structure of matter. There have of course been new great syntheses, consolidations and unifications in which the unity-seeking heart of Froebel would rejoice. However, it would be extremely difficult now, in the light of all the history of our knowledge during the last hundred years, to regard the simple crystallographic facts and laws which so impressed themselves on Froebel's mind, or even the more general mathematical schemes with which they can be linked, as more than one aspect of an immensely more complicated and less reducible and simplifiable world. If unity there ultimately is, the way to

it has become far more roundabout and, at least intellectually, far less assured and self-sufficient.

2. We have also widened beyond recognition our knowledge of the human race and its varieties of life and beliefs and practices. Both anthropology and prehistoric archaeology have opened up to us new dimensions of information, understanding and insight, and have made impossible the Europe-centred and indeed nineteenth-century-Europe-centred naivety of a standpoint such as Froebel's. We can now only think of our culture as one out of many, both in time and in space, and if we can find grounds for, nevertheless, reaffirming its values and outlook, we can but do so, soberly and even diffidently, as apparently the most reasonable choice on balance that is available to us up to the present. And if we choose it, that is, in fact, because it is the one historic culture which has sought to explore and understand and learn from all others, and at the same time to open its doors wide to every avenue of potential further learning and growth.

3. Finally, we have lived through another hundred years of chequered history since Froebel's death, including two world wars, an incredible tempo of technological progress, the shrinkage of all our diverse human societies (through modern industry, trade and communications) into a single interdependent whole, and a far-reaching revolution in our political, social and economic perspective. Here again we must say that Froebel lived in a somewhat narrow world. His treatment, to take one example, of domestics as a lower species from whose debasing influence children had at all costs to be saved; his exclusive concentration, in the Education of Man, on the upbringing of boys, and his restricted social horizon generally were a limitation on his equipment and vision as an educator even in his own age. Today much of his educational philosophy, in its social aspect, might well

appear almost absurdly unrelated to many of the urgent problems of our time. Froebel's direct ascent from little Thuringian children in their Keilhau setting straight to the universe leaves out far too many alternative roads, as well as all the crucial intermediate steps.

4

ANSWER TO THE PROBLEM: THE VALIDITY OF FROEBEL'S PHILOSOPHY OF EDUCATION FOR FREEDOM

XII

To what conclusion now are we brought? It is important to emphasise once more that although Froebel's picture of the child is in many ways mistaken, this is so always by incompleteness rather than by inherent error. It is all light and no shade (or such shade as cannot be denied is regarded only as wantonly brought in from outside); yet all the elements of light are real and highly significant. The "shade" element must be filled in and is itself fundamental. Much of it is assuredly inborn, and though much may perhaps arise only from the child's early condition and experiences, even this becomes so inevitably and deeply interwoven with the whole fabric of his personality that we must just accept it as part of the groundwork on which we have to build. Nevertheless it is true, and far more true than we usually allow, that there is that in the child which does seek to learn and understand, to explore and discover, to express and create, to develop and grow; and there is that in him also which constantly gropes for inward unity and integration, for social harmony and co-operation, for communion and solidarity. Only there are strong contrary forces as well, powerful obstacles and limitations, conflicts and divisions, and an infinity of ways in which the positive forces may be weakened or arrested or led astray.

That, I have suggested, is the real picture from which our educational philosophy must start, and it will not of itself support the beliefs and hopes of Froebel's approach. We cannot, if we would, just leave the child free to grow; in his earliest days, we, but above all his mother, are unavoidably gods who rule and dominate his growth. In so far as later on we can leave him free, or can seem to do so, there is no guarantee, and only an imperfect prospect, that he will grow healthily and happily, to say nothing of unfolding straight into his divine destiny. And even if, following Froebel himself, we do, after all, take an active part in steering his growth, through *Mutter und Koselieder*, Gifts and Occupations, and so right on, what we can achieve is very limited and, if we rely too much on this particular scheme, apt to be more apparent than real. And whatever more we might need to say, it is certain that the large element of factual insufficiency and error in Froebel's educational doctrine must frustrate *his* purposes and defeat *his* hopes.

What would he himself make of this conclusion? Could he resist it, once he has adopted the goal of the child's own growth, invoked the criterion of his own response, and insisted, as a prerequisite, on our disinterested and devoted study of him? Has he not in fact firmly pledged himself to accept whatever this study brings? But if he accepted the conclusion, where would he, or could he, go from there? It seems that he could not choose but reconsider, and at least partly revise, his basic worldvision itself. Perhaps the changes required would not be very great; perhaps in the end only a much more complex and roundabout pattern of realisation of the divine. Or perhaps he would be led to stress much more that divine help from without (brought of course through the vehicle of the family and the community) which a more active and historical interpretation of Christianity might provide. Perhaps he would find a solution in something like Mr. Hamilton's view, with its room for shade as well as light, but its conservation, nevertheless, of all the main lineaments of Froebel's own educational gospel.

These are matters for speculation. It is tempting for those of us who (on whatever grounds) share his chief educational values to believe that he could not have done other than to maintain these. That fundamental attitude of respect for the child, respect for his personality and integrity, and, above all, for his right to be treated as an end in himself: that is a conquest from which, once it has been achieved, no one would be willing to turn back. We can indeed hold that this attitude was something so profoundly rooted in the deepest needs and cravings of his own childhood that nothing could possibly uproot it; that his very philosophy had been shaped by the same needs, and was thus a supporting frame for his educational creed rather than the source on which this depended; and that therefore it would not be this creed but the philosophy which would in fact be recast. But if we were to take this latter ground, we should be open to an obvious retort. Why should not the philosophy—the testimony to and belief in the divine as such—have its own elemental roots? Why should it not be this that expressed what was deepest and strongest in Froebel, so that in any conflict it would be this that prevailed? Such a view might find confirmation first in his passionate apostolic urge and secondly in its translation into that eager, pressing didactic impulse which so visibly shaped the main features of his later educational scheme. At an inescapable parting of the ways these forces might, after all, have carried him quite far into the field of some modified *remoulding* and regenerative theory of education.

XIII

Such speculations may be interesting, but they cannot be very profitable. All that can be said is that ultimate philosophy and educational philosophy must cohere if both are not to become meaningless. If their cohesion is ruptured, some way must be found of restoring it, whether from one end or from the other, or by convergent changes in both. But only Froebel could decide what would constitute a satisfying mode of restoration for Froebel. And that is not, after all, now our main problem. The problem to which we now come back in sharper form, given this whole which no longer fits together, is not Froebel's but our own. If the whole breaks down (at least in Froebel's form) because of the conflicting facts, how far can we still uphold its educational part? And, above all, in so far as we do, on what grounds different from his own do we do so? How far indeed do those of us who are still ready to range ourselves with his main educational principles do so on the same grounds—or in the same sense?

These are not, I believe, over-subtle theoretical questions, but vitally important practical ones. It seems to me not the least of Froebel's contributions to educational thought that he obliges us to face them. By directly presenting his educational philosophy as derived from his ultimate world-view, he leaves us no choice but to acknowledge the same unavoidable relationship between our attitude to his educational doctrine and *our* world-view. This accordingly forces us to think about the relations between our varying attitudes to Froebel on the one hand and our world-views on the other. And so something which is much too often left all too vague and undefined and unthought-out is brought into the open, and we can see everything it implies, and the fundamental problem, to first appearance almost insoluble, which we are thus set. Whereupon we find in the end that, as I

have already suggested, it is Froebel's educational doctrine, seen in a new light now, which provides us with
our nearest approach to a solution.

XIV

The way to this conclusion is not too easy or simple,
and can be only very inadequately sketched within the
scope of the present essay; but I believe it is essential to
make the attempt to trace it.

The first stage is, I think, to work out still more fully
the total impasse to which our argument would seem to
lead. If every educational philosophy is finally caught
up in the unresolved clash of ultimate philosophies, we
are left without any agreed common measure at all.
What remains is a confusion of different ultimate beliefs
each pursuing its own course. Many of us may be ready
to reaffirm most of Froebel's central educational doctrines, but we each of us do so for our own reasons and
only as far as they fit into our own personal creeds. Except in so far as we do happen to share the same ultimate
creeds, our semblance of agreement is merely illusory,
like that of separate curves based on different laws which
over a limited segment seem to coincide. If we look more
closely, we can see that that is solely because we have not
measured this segment accurately enough or pursued it
far enough. As soon as we do so, the semblance of agreement breaks down; we are thrown back on our disparate
and incommensurable individual curves. Each is a law
only to itself, without validity for the others. And under
these conditions, the very idea of shared or common
progress along a common road must disintegrate; the
word may remain, but it will mean something different
for each person who applies it. For each it can signify
only the measure of approach to his particular philosophic goal or aims. Any coinciding or nearly coinciding
segment will be hailed as "progress" by all those travel-

ling along it, but by each solely in terms of his own final course; and each of us will inevitably qualify the term, or withdraw it altogether from others, as soon as any deviation from his curve appears. In other words, behind the façade of an apparent common language and a common measure, the real underlying reality will be an anarchy which is ultimate and incurable.

This of course is an extreme picture and perhaps no one would accept it as it stands. However, whilst many people will feel that it is not true or, at any rate, very much overstated, others might well wish to emphasise that in so far as it is true, it represents either something in itself eminently valuable or at worst the obverse side of what we must regard in that light. A wide range of different beliefs freely expressed and developed is the natural expression of an independent community leading a vigorous intellectual life. Moreover, the healthier and more vigorous this life, the more actively and consistently and fully each belief will be taken up and worked out, thus in turn serving to carry that life forward. That is the way in which different beliefs can best be judged, can best make their own contribution, and can best promote the growth of our insight and understanding as a whole. The constant mutual scrutiny and criticism and contest of differing beliefs, each free to try out its utmost strength against all the others, is the great process from which truth and progress spring. This holds as much in the educational field as in every other, and is as valuable and life-giving there. If it is correct that different philosophies can be carried to a point where they no longer accept one another's most elemental criteria of judgment so that the clash between them becomes incapable of being resolved, this may truly be a reduction to anarchy. But it is an extreme and exceptional case which does not detract from a vast deal of genuine shared progress and widening agreement; and at the worst it is a price which we must be content to pay for that priceless individual and social good, the great principle of freedom of thought on which most that we most value in our civilisation depends.

XV

I have stated both sides of the foregoing argument in their most uncompromising form. There is matter here in turn for unending debate, but I wish to suggest a different approach which I think *can* lead to a special kind of concord. It is clear, however, now that our discussion cannot be confined to the educational field. Since our educational philosophies (in so far as we have any) are bound up with our total philosophies, we find ourselves inevitably carried into the conflict between these in the wider field of our social history at large. And there we must note that something more is involved than the genteel anarchy of our educational discussions. For these the ring is kept by the general rules of tolerance and compromise and avoidance of extremes which have become the established practice of our society. But these themselves, in this larger realm, are far from secure. We have indeed been slowly and painfully building up over the last two hundred years that general principle of the freedom of thought on which our rules of mutual tolerance and forbearance ultimately rest. That principle had first to make its way against excessively zealous and fanatical forms of religion seeking to establish their universal and absolute sway; so that for a long time the very notion of freedom of thought seemed to signify freedom to depart (as far as ever one felt impelled) from the prevailing religious beliefs. But the principle, once accepted, led to an immense proliferation of divergent beliefs, including every possible kind of non-religious, anti-religious and anarchic ones, and so to an unlimited clash of differing philosophies and creeds. And this clash has in turn not remained merely theoretical, nor stayed within the bounds of the principle of freedom of thought which had made it possible. It has generated new threats against that principle more formidable in many ways than any that have gone before. And at the core of those threats there lies that final anarchy to which I have referred, itself turned into an ultimate principle. In our own time we have now been faced twice with urgent danger from two of these extreme forms of offspring of secular freedom of thought which strive to devour their parent. In both cases they are creeds, or as we nowadays call them, ideologies, which acknowledge no truth, no criterion and no principle outside themselves. For them there is no arbitrament but force and power. They are group-creeds by which those who hold them seek to achieve absolute power, either because they believe in nothing but those ideas plus power, or because at bottom they believe in nothing but power. We have, almost too late, struggled against and overcome the first of these threats, from Nazism-Fascism. We are now engaged in struggling, we hope not too late, against the second, the pseudo-Communism or power-Communism of Moscow. Both these struggles demonstrate, if a demonstration is needed, that the peril from an unresolved and unresolvable clash of ultimate philosophies can be only too real. It is, as I have urged, not something merely theoretical, nor something wholly admirable, nor something to be too readily accepted as inevitable and only the price we have to pay for the great social good of the freedom of thought which we have so successfully struggled to achieve. For the simple fact is that, so long as the clash of philosophies can take such forms as it has done in Nazism and power-Communism and attain the wide and powerful initial momentum which both have secured, we have not remotely achieved that good.

XVI

What now has all this to do with Froebel? I hope to show immensely much. The struggle against Nazism-Fascism, and now against Moscow pseudo-Communism, has for many of us brought into a new focus that primary value of freedom—freedom of thought and of way of life —which they so dangerously menace. We should like, indeed, to think that we are *all* agreed upon it; but of course we are not. Nazis, Fascists and pseudo-Communists certainly are not, and they constantly make new converts. All that we can say is that *the great majority of us*, even if we otherwise hold very different ultimate creeds, do agree upon that one value, and accept in common the primary need to maintain and defend it. Why do we do so, and why, if we are a great majority, as most of us believe, have we only succeeded so imperfectly and do we remain so much at the mercy of one threat to it after another?

The issues raised by these questions are not to be exhausted in the present limited essay. But I think one main aspect of them falls directly within its theme. I believe that our current theory of freedom as a whole is not sufficiently clearly thought out and, for that reason, not adequately founded. And the more adequate foundation we need still waits for the realisation of the ideas for which Froebel stood. His educational philosophy provides (even if not quite in the way he had conceived) the true groundwork for an effective theory of freedom.

The first point to emphasise is that we believe in freedom in a different sense, or at least in an additional one, to that in which we believe in our other basic values. There is a sense in which we *agree* to accept the value of freedom. We come together, as it were, to do so; it provides the common ground on which we all can meet— and on which, indeed, we must meet. Our willingness to agree on this is the condition on which alone we can be secure in all our other and differing beliefs. In other words, agreement here is not dependent on processes of logic or demonstrative argument, which in fact have never proved sufficient. It represents a common by-passing of these processes because of our recognition of a common urgent need, which otherwise there can be no assurance of satisfying. If we want to be allowed, each one of us, to think as we must and live as we feel impelled, however differently from one another, we must work out together a certain limited body of shared belief to safeguard us all. And the essence of this, as we know, is precisely the principle of freedom—freedom of thought and conscience, expression and practice and of every way of life within the boundaries, for each of us, of consonance with the equal freedom of all others.

Of course it remains true that this acceptance of freedom as a common value must be at least *compatible* with the nature of our individual ultimate beliefs. It is far better still, for the security of our common value, if it directly *follows* from our ultimate beliefs, however different these may otherwise be. But that is not essential; compatibility is enough, because our common need is so manifest and so great.

The next point, however, is that this special status of the value of freedom carries its own limitations and its own special requirements with it. Our belief in freedom is in a peculiar sense a voluntary belief, accepted in common for a vital purpose. To achieve this purpose it must be effective. It must be stable, it must be sufficient, and it must be fully worked out so that the freedom we need is truly secured. It must, in fact, start from an adequate notion of freedom in ourselves. But these conditions are currently far from being fulfilled. Our conventional ideas of freedom mean too little and are applied too late. As historically developed and transmitted, they have been primarily notions of non-coercion and non-interference;

of *leaving* "free"; of letting alone and *laisser faire*. They have, indeed, long been criticised on the ground of their insufficiency, their negativeness and emptiness, in the political and, above all, in the economic spheres. But we are less aware how wide open they are to an even more radical order of criticism. This is essentially psychological and comes out most clearly in the realm of education.

Here, indeed, the significant fact is that the very concept of freedom, as conventionally interpreted, has been regarded as applicable only to the parent, not to the child. In relation to the latter, that concept was quite compatible even with interference and coercion—and for the most part rested on these. The fight for freedom was the fight for the parent's right to have his children educated in a way chosen by him, according to his beliefs or creed, and not under the control of a particular "official" religion. This, however, meant most often merely that parents could set up or choose group-schools in which their particular creeds were, by every time-honoured method, inculcated in the child.

It is clear enough that we can find no foundation here for such a conception of freedom as our argument requires. If this is to represent a common value in which we all, by deliberate and free agreement, meet, it calls for something very different in ourselves from the mere idea of non-coercion and non-interference as traditionally conceived. It must stand for a positive and fully formed inward reality, proceeding out of clear vision and balanced understanding and grasp. And that is not something which can be conferred on us from without by legislative enactment, or which can be relied upon to descend on us suddenly together with our right to vote.

XVII

In effect, what is essential, if we are to be capable of the freedom which on any adequate social theory we

need, is a philosophy of *education for freedom from the start*.
That is the great Froebelian revolution. Capacity for
freedom is something which, step by step, must be built
up in us. It must represent a progressive and cumulative
achievement carried forward by growth itself. Education
in freedom and by freedom are essential for it, but they
are simply means. The end is that education from within,
by the child's own many-sided experience and activity continually integrated into harmonious development, which
will carry him to adulthood as fully master of himself and
an autonomous and responsible member of a free society.

Such an educational philosophy is then simply the
carrying to completion of the freely elected common
philosophy of freedom which is our most urgent social
need. It no longer depends on any particular set of
ultimate metaphysical beliefs (whether Froebel's or any
other), but provides the fundamental platform on which
the most diverse ultimate beliefs, so long only as they are
compatible with tolerance of one another, can meet. And
once we assume the shared value of freedom, we can
confine our concern, if we wish, to the pragmatic minimum of the contrast between those conditions which will
effectively safeguard it and those which, whatever
nominal homage we may pay to it, leave it precarious
and insecure. At the best, freedom from coercion and
interference in adult life comes, as we have said, too late;
after living through most of our formative period from
infancy to adolescence under conditions of coercion and
interference, too few of us come out inwardly capable of
being free. What is even more fatal perhaps than positive
educational impositions from without is the *habitual disregard*, in our conventional traditions of upbringing, of
the demands of inward integration and growth; the lack
of access to wide ranges of human experience; the lack
of exercise in methods of judgment and decision; the
failure to provide *equipment for freedom and choice*. Those

who have been left through their plastic period to the fortuitous interplay of coercion and neglect, disregard, privation and frustration, and every sort of unregulated force within and without, will be only too apt to emerge at the mercy of every further strong current they may meet. This is in fact demonstrated by the ease with which even the external freedom that is one's adult "birthright" is surrendered or lost under the play of one or another form of propaganda or mass-movement or mob-appeal. That is the soil in which power-ideologies or creeds flourish, though in the end they may destroy even most of those who embrace them.

However, the positive conditions of freedom amount to something very much larger than any mere sum of avoidances of failures or mistakes. And the inspiration to a philosophy of education for freedom lies for most of us deeper than the mere need to make our freedom secure in later life, vital though that may be. Both this need and those deeper demands are perhaps most satisfyingly met by Froebel's own fundamental principle: full respect for the integrity and individuality of every child. That most searching of moralists Immanuel Kant saw the supreme ethical law in the principle: treat every human being as an end in himself. But most if not all ethics is pivoted on the so-called "moral subject", either taken for granted or formally declared to be the responsible adult. We may, I think, account it Froebel's greatest revolution that he extended and deepened and transformed this principle by insisting that we must treat not merely every adult but every *child* as an end in himself. And every youngest child, every infant practically from the start. In this way, and this way only, respect for the integrity and individuality of every human person can be built into all the relations of adults to him and into the whole planning and process of education from the outset; and the requisite range of opportunity, the equipment and the capacity and power for freedom will then be seen as part of the very birthright of every child.

We need not greatly elaborate here the theory of education which flows out of the above principles, since in fact most of it is in Froebel and the rest follows self-evidently. We need only say, in the most general terms, that *range of opportunity* signifies access, by all the means of appreciation as well as understanding and creation, to the whole human heritage. *Equipment and capacity for freedom* means skills and trained aptitudes; the amplest exercise in discrimination and judgment; and, above all, the mastery of methods and criteria in the great world of exploration, learning and discovery. *Power of choice* means an integrated wholeness of character and personality which knows what it seeks and why it seeks this, and is thus capable of firm and clear, mutually accordant and cumulative decisions. The key throughout lies in the crucial child-centred principles of experience and activity, integration and growth. The principles, however, must be construed all the time socially as much as individually, since, first, they apply equally to every child, and therefore their application to each must continually be so modulated as to harmonise with the equal benefit of all. And secondly human growth is into and through a community, and indeed in the end the human community, the adventure and growth of the race. The optimum of equipped and powered freedom can only be freedom within a community, and all the main ways of appreciation, enjoyment, understanding and creation rest upon social co-operation and can only flourish through it. Education for freedom aims at fully responsive as well as responsible members of society: microcosms who reflect, but reflect individually, up to the limit of their capacity, the achievements, the perspectives and the possibilities of the race, which each of them may carry a step farther along its way.

All this can only be catalogued here, but just adds up once again to the education of the whole man, in individual and social unity and harmony. The great difference which arises out of the true psychological facts about the child is that what for Froebel was a solution, for the modern Froebelian educator merely lays down the terms of his problem. Those are the directions and the goals to be aimed at. But he must start from something very different, and yet may use only methods which are consonant with those directions and those goals. His end is within the child, and his criteria must always be the latter's actual response and development and advance. The child has, indeed, in him the forces and motives which can lead by those methods in those directions to those goals. But there are also all the contrary forces, the inertias and the limitations. The educator must continually strive to foster and co-operate with the former and to overcome the latter. His task is an intensely difficult, even if it is also an intensely rewarding, one. He is a navigator engaged on a very long voyage in uncertain seas, though if nothing goes seriously wrong he can all the time note progress and hearten himself with it. But he may not relax: he must constantly anew seek out favouring winds and currents; avoid reefs, stagnant backwaters and whirlpools, and often enough make his way with great difficulty through gales and storms.

Moreover, every child involves a new voyage and new problems. For the aims and methods which the Froebelian educator imposes on himself, there are no general or permanent solutions. There must be no small degree of new study and new adaptation in every new case; each child is an individual entitled to individual respect and freedom, and posing his own new problems about the way he can best be brought to individual and social fulfilment. Furthermore, aspirations like the maximum of opportunity and stimulus for every child, and the utmost freedom for each compatible with equal scope for all, must indeed be set up as guiding aims and criteria, but in practice they provide no ready-made programme in themselves but merely signify the most difficult tasks of selection and rejection, withholding and intervention. There is never, moreover, any certainty about the rightness of the solution; only time, and often far-off time, can tell. Most often, in fact, optimal rightness is by the nature of the case excluded, because the educator must deal with a group of children and nothing can conceivably ensure perfect adaptation to *all* their differing (and often incompatible) requirements *all* the time.

Nor does all this exhaust the problems of the "free" educator. He is, as we have seen, not concerned only with universal principles and individual children, but has to learn to take into account also their natural groupings according to degrees of capacity, their differences in special endowments and bents, and all their divergences in temperament and personality. And furthermore he has finally to accept, however much he struggles against them, the well-nigh fatal limitations imposed on him by all the cramping social and economic and cultural conditions within which concrete educational processes are inevitably cast. These far too often make an adequate realisation of *his* aims by *his* methods quite impossible; he must just struggle as far as he can along his road, whilst in his other capacities he strives and hopes for such changes in those surroundings as will gradually allow more fruitfulness to his work.

XVIII

However, the "free" educator, who knows what he seeks to do and why, will struggle on his path undeterred. He will remain aware that though the way of education for freedom is the hard way, it is the only one which can claim intrinsic meaning and value, and the only way which can eventually lead to individuals and a society that are worth while in their own right independently of anything outside themselves. He may perhaps hope for much more than that. He may have some ultimate vision which he believes can thus, and only thus, be brought to realisation. Indeed, it may remain an essential part of his aim that the children in his charge, by the right experience and the right understanding, shall themselves be led to this same vision. Clearly those educators who believe that their community has already found the true way of life cannot do other than open up for their children any roads which may guide them to this. The spirit of the Froebelian ideal of education for freedom, as here interpreted, demands only that the aim and touchstone shall always remain within the child. It must be his own experience, his own free advance in understanding and acceptance, and his own final choice that counts; and of course if this is to count he needs also the opportunity of experiencing and understanding alternative visions and ways of life, since only thus can he make a genuinely free choice.

On the other hand, there are not only those who have their own ultimate vision, or perhaps rather diverse approaches to the same vision, as so many of them would today believe. There are also many for whom freedom to decide their own ultimate beliefs only means freedom not to decide at all and not to advance (according to their own inward law) beyond a great question-mark. For them, however, this freedom must count more than ever as the final *reachable* value; and the philosophy of education for freedom and of free individual human beings as ends in themselves must, just because for them there are no established ends beyond this, represent the last assured word. Because freedom of thought is peculiarly necessary and valuable to them, they have, in fact, been among the main protagonists of the ideal of education in and by and for freedom since Froebel's times. Among those in this group who have done most to work out all the implications of this ideal both for the individual and for society —and, above all, for the former as an integral part of the latter—the name which stands out is that of Professor Dewey. In Great Britain the same values have been powerfully represented throughout his work by Earl Russell, who has indeed sought to translate them into his own practical educational applications. But they have perhaps been most furthered here by the late Susan Isaacs, who has probably done more than anyone in our day to gain for them a wide currency and acceptance in many fertile forms of psychological and educational illumination and guidance.

Members of this group, who might, I suppose, be described as philosophic agnostics and educational humanists, are in a sense the exception that proves the rule, because their educational philosophy cannot derive from any ultimate set of positive philosophic beliefs. The rule is preserved because their educational creed rests upon the *absence* of such beliefs and builds on this very fact its own provisional ideals. These, as we have seen, are the ideals of freedom to believe or disbelieve; of the end-value of each human being as the one value that is left; and of the self-justifying aim for each human being equally, and so for all, of their greatest possible realisation and fulfilment. This must mean the utmost participation open to each in everything which, by exploration and construction and appreciation and creation, the human race has so far been able to achieve, and the utmost conservation and further development of this heritage for the participation of its future heirs. But such a creed of active and creative life signifies at the same time for everyone the true maximum of zest and happiness open to human being as such; for, as Blake so truly saw, energy is eternal delight.

That is one way of putting the case from a philosophic-agnostic point of view; some of its upholders might choose other ways, and the writer can only in the last resort speak for himself. The point here is merely to illustrate the form which the Froebelian ideal of education, as I think we can still rightly call it, might take in the hands of such of us as are far away from his own ultimate world-vision. For even in this form its central core is still the insistence that every human being, even the youngest child, shall be respected as an end in himself, and, so long as he stays dependent on us, shall be served as such. I have tried to indicate how much this implies. Froebel retains for modern progressive education the significance of a great pioneer, because his essential principles are still so largely unrealised, and because history has shown how vital it is for us all that the work of education for freedom shall be truly done.

BIBLIOGRAPHY

The following short list represents a few selected titles of books bearing on the subject of this volume. For fuller study the library of the National Froebel Foundation at 2 Manchester Square, London, may be consulted.

Froebel's own writings

The Education of Man, Froebel. W. N. Hailmann. (An abridged translation, with analytical index, comments and synopsis.)
Appleton, 1906

Die Menschenerziehung, Friedrich Froebel. Herausgegeben von Dr. Wichard Lange. Berlin 1863

Ausgewählte Schriften, Friedrich Froebel. Band I *Kleine Schriften und Briefe, 1809–1851*, Band II, *Menschenerziehung.* Herausgegeben von Erika Hoffmann.
Verlag Helmut Kupper, Godesberg 1951

Pedagogics of the Kindergarten, Froebel. Trans. Josephine Jarvis.
Appleton, 1907

Kindergartenwesen, Friedrich Froebel. Pichler, Wien 1883

Autobiography of Friedrich Froebel. Trans. E. Michaelis and H. K. Moore. Swan Sonnenschein, 1886

Letters on the Kindergarten, Friedrich Froebel. Trans. E. Michaelis and H. K. Moore. Swan Sonnenschein, 1891

Mother's Songs, Games and Stories (*Mutter und Kose-Lieder*), Friedrich Froebel, Trans. Frances and Emily Lord.
Rice, London 1920

Froebel and the Kindergarten

Friedrich Fröbel, J. Prufer. Teubner, Leipzig 1920

Froebel and Education by Self Activity, H. Courthope Bowen. Great Educators Series. Heinemann, 1893

Reminiscences of Friedrich Froebel, Baroness B. von Marenholtz-Bülow. Trans. Mrs. Horace Mann.
Lee & Shepard, Boston 1895

Kindergarten Practice, Parts I and II. Koehler's *Praxis des Kindergartens*. Trans. and abridged by Mary Gurney.
Myers, London 1877

Papers on Froebel's Kindergarten, Barnard, Henry (Ed.).
American Froebel Union Edition, 1881

The Students' Froebel, W. H. Herford.   Isbister, 1901

Essays on Educational Reformers, R. H. Quick. Longmans, 1898

The Kindergarten Principles of Froebel's System, Emily Shirreff.
Swan Sonnenschein, 1897

The Kindergarten at Home, Emily Shirreff.   Clive (no date)

The Paradise of Childhood, Edward Wiebe. Quarter Century Edition.   Phillip, 1896

Froebel's Kindergarten Principles, W. H. Kilpatrick.
MacMillan, New York 1916

Sketches of Froebel's Life and Times, Introduction by W. J. Claxton.   Milton Bradley, Springfield, Mass. 1914

The Kindergarten in American Education, N. C. Vandewalker.
MacMillan, 1908

A Practical Guide to the English Kindergarten, J. and B. Ronge.
Myers, 1884

Educational History

Lectures on the History of Education, Joseph Payne.
Longmans, 1892

The Growth of Freedom in Education, W. J. McCallister.
Constable, 1931

A History of Infant Education, R. R. Rusk.
University of London Press, 1933

A History of the Education of Young Children, T. Raymont.
Longmans, 1937

The Story of Infant Schools and Kindergartens, E. R. Murray.
Pitman (no date)

Ladybarn House and the Work of W. H. Herford, W. C. R. Hicks.
Manchester University Press, 1936

The Diary of a Free Kindergarten, Lileen Hardy.
Gay & Hancock, 1912

Dickens as an Educator, James L. Hughes.   Arnold, 1901

The Story of Camden House School, M. E. Nuth.
George Pulman, 1950

Margaret McMillan, Albert Mansbridge.   Dent, 1932

Method

The Camp School, Margaret McMillan. Allen & Unwin, 1917

The Project Method, W. H. Kilpatrick.
Teacher's College, Columbia University, 1929

The School and Society, John Dewey.
Cambridge University Press, 1936

The School and the Child, John Dewey.   Blackie, 1906

The Dewey School, John Dewey, 1900.
Revised edition Froebel Society, 1929

The Decroly Class, A. Hamaïde.   Dent, 1925

The New Era in the Junior School, E. B. Warr.   Methuen, 1937

Froebel Education To-day, O. Barbara Priestman.
University of London Press, 1946

Hadow Reports. Infant and Nursery Schools.
The Primary School.

Basic Requirements of the Junior School, prepared by the North-Eastern Junior Schools Association.
University of London Press, 1949

Junior School Community, M. Atkinson.   Longmans, 1949

Learning and Teaching in the Junior School.   Methuen, 1947

Activity in the Primary School, M. V. Daniel.   Blackwell, 1947

Life in the Nursery School, L. de Lissa.   Longmans, 1949

Testing Results in the Infant School, D. E. M. Gardner.
Methuen, 1948

Long Term Results of Infant School Methods, D. E. M. Gardner.
Methuen, 1950

Exploration in the Junior School, H. Philips and F. J. C. McInnes.   University of London Press, 1950

Education through Experience in the Infant School Years, Edna Mellor.   Blackwell, 1950

Play in the Infants' School, E. R. Boyce.   Methuen, 1946

Psychology

The First Five Years of Life, A. Gesell.   Methuen, 1950

The Child from Five to Ten, A. Gesell and F. L. Ilg.
                    H. Hamilton, 1946

Intellectual Growth in Young Children, Susan Isaacs.
                    Routledge, 1930

Social Development in Young Children, Susan Isaacs.
                    Routledge, 1933

Troubles of Children and Parents, Susan Isaacs. Methuen, 1948

The Development of Learning in Young Children, L. C. Wagoner.
                    McGraw Hill, 1933

Social and Emotional Development of the Pre-School Child, K. Bridges.   Kegan Paul, 1931

Social Behaviour and Child Personality, Lois B. Murphy.
                    Columbia University Press, 1937

APPENDIX

Froebel's Gifts and Occupations

Gift I

Box of six worsted balls of 1½-inch diameter, red, yellow, blue, orange, green, violet.

Gift II

Box containing a cube, a cylinder and a ball of 1½-inch diameter, with suspending frame.

Gift III

Box containing a 2-inch cube, divided once in every direction, forming eight small cubes of 1 inch.

Gift IV

Box containing a 2-inch cube, divided into eight solid oblongs, 2 inches × 1 inch × ½ inch.

Gift V

Box containing a 3-inch cube, divided twice in each direction, forming twenty-seven 1-inch cubes, three of which are divided into halves, and three into quarters.

Gift VI

Box containing a 3-inch cube, divided to form twenty-seven solid oblongs, of which three are divided into halves to form four-sided prisms, and six into halves to form square half-cubes.

Occupations

1 Tablet laying. Square and triangular planes of polished wood of two colours, for constructing designs.
2 Paper folding; 4-inch squares and hexagons of assorted colours, also larger sheets of white and coloured paper.

3 Paper cutting: material as above.

4 Paper plaiting or weaving. Coloured paper in the form of strips, and bases for interweaving.

5 Paper twisting. Paper and cardboard strips of different widths.

6 Stick plaiting. Smooth and flexible strips of wood 10 inches long.

7 Stick laying. Round and quadrangular sticks 12 inches long.

8 Pea work. Small pointed sticks for joining together soaked and softened peas, to form skeleton three-dimensional constructions.

9 Wood and cork work. Corks, pointed sticks and wires.

10 Ring laying. Metal rings of different sizes and segments of these.

11 Thread laying. 12- and 18-inch soft cotton threads to be used as lines to form curved designs.

12 Drawing. Chequered paper and books.

13 Pricking. White and coloured cardboard and paper, chequered paper; pricking needle with handle.

14 Sewing. Coloured wools, silks and cottons. Perforated cards with pictures, patterns, letters, maps, etc. Cardboard objects to be decorated with embroidery, etc.

MISCELLANEOUS. Painting, drawing, clay modelling, sand modelling, ravelling bunting, bead threading, Japanese straw-work, basketry, cane weaving, stencilling.

The above particulars are summarised from the publisher's catalogue in Mary Gurney's "Kindergarten Practice", 1877.

INDEX

240